The Coffeehouse Investor's Ground Rules

The Coffeehouse Investor's Ground Rules

Save, Invest, and Plan for a Life of Wealth and Happiness

Bill Schultheis

WILEY

Published by John Wiley & Sons, Inc., Hoboken, New Jersey.
Published simultaneously in Canada.

For general information on our other products and services or for technical support, please contact our Customer Care Department within the United States at (800) 762–2974, outside the United States at (317) 572–3993, or fax (317) 572–4002.

Wiley publishes in a variety of print and electronic formats and by print-on-demand. Some material included with standard print versions of this book may not be included in e-books or in print-on-demand. If this book refers to media such as a CD or DVD that is not included in the version you purchased, you may download this material at http://booksupport.wiley.com. For more information about Wiley products, visit www.wiley.com.

Library of Congress Cataloging-in-Publication Data is Available:
ISBN 9781119717089 (Hardcover)
ISBN 9781119718055 (ePDF)
ISBN 9781119717119 (ePub)

COVER DESIGN & ARTWORK: PAUL McCARTH

Printed in the United States of America.

SKY10021801_101920

Contents

Foreword

Bill Schultheis starts his book with a simple reflection: *We are changing the world, one investor at a time.* Over the past 20 years, on countless exchanges I have had with Bill – in person, over the telephone, and through our emails – as we discover new and better ways to help investors reach their lifetime goals, we always seem to end by voicing the same intention.

We are changing the world, one investor at a time.

Our connection goes all the way back to 1998. That was the year I wrote my first book, *The Only Guide to a Winning Investment Strategy You'll Ever Need.* That was the same year Bill wrote his first book, *The Coffeehouse Investor – How to Build Wealth, Ignore Wall Street, and Get On with Your Life.*

Our books had at least three things in common: both attempted to explain complex investing concepts in a layman's manner; both highlighted the wisdom of capturing market returns through index funds; and both were published in the middle of a raging bull market fueled by the dot-com boom, when few investors paid much attention to efficient markets and index funds.

The bear market that followed was the catalyst for investors to seek out a smarter way to build portfolios. We were prepared with the solution.

Bill Schultheis possesses the unique gift of simplicity in his writing. He takes dense financial terms bandied about on Wall Street and turns them upside down, so that after reading his work, you turn away from standard deviations, alphas and betas, to focus instead on wealth-building components that matter most of all in life.

For this reason, my firm, Buckingham Strategic Wealth, invited him to St. Louis in 2001, to speak to our clients. True to his book, Bill's presentation of stocks, bonds, and asset allocation evolved into a deeper exploration of using your financial resources to live a more meaningful life.

The late Jack Bogle spoke of the "missionary zeal" that he hoped to inspire, of taking the time to share with others the simple tenet of using index funds as building blocks for portfolios.

When I reflect on the past 20 years, Bill is near the top of a luminous list of authors, advisors, and academics in his passion for carrying on the work of America's legendary stalwart.

Our shared investing experience is based on decades of financial research, showing that markets are efficient. In an investing world consumed with owning the top stocks of leading industries, building lasting wealth requires a patient commitment to capturing the returns of global markets.

The investing process, however, is only one component, albeit an important one, to building lasting financial wealth. As Bill vigorously points out in this book, the primary benefit to embracing efficient markets in portfolio construction is that investors are emotionally freed to turn away from random, short-term volatility of markets, and focus on financial planning issues that are essential to lifetime wealth accumulation.

This is especially true for women, as Bill points out in Chapter 3. According to the consulting firm McKinsey & Company, a vast transfer of wealth is unfolding, as male baby boomers die, leaving assets to spouses for their control and management. It is estimated that by 2030, women will be in charge of $30 trillion, an increase from $10 trillion in 2016.[1]

Bill Schultheis is uniquely qualified to discuss the challenges investors face in building lasting wealth. Working as co-owner and advisor of Soundmark Wealth Management in Seattle, Washington, he sees the same complexities faced by clients of Buckingham Strategic Wealth, of integrating tax-management solutions within the portfolio design of your comprehensive financial plan.

For 20 years our investing and financial planning discussions always seem to move to conversations about life. Bill has always pushed me to climb the mountains of the Pacific Northwest. I encouraged him to join me rafting the white waters of the Colorado River.

There comes a point in white-water rafting (and Bill has shared the same in his mountain-climbing experience), when you are in the danger zone; you have to slow the mind down, focus on what is at hand, breathe, and push on.

That is the experience facing the investor today. The global economy is in turmoil from the virus pandemic. Interest rates are at an all-time low. The Federal Reserve is flooding the economy

[1]Baghai, P., Howard, O., Prakash, L., and Zucker, J. (2020). Women as the next wave of growth in US wealth management. McKinsey & Company, July 29. https://www.mckinsey.com/industries/financial-services/our-insights/women-as-the-next-wave-of-growth-in-us-wealth-management#.

with money with the fear of inflation emerging. Significant tax law changes loom large on the horizon. Wall Street is inundating unsuspecting investors with meaningless and expensive financial products.

It is time for investors to slow down, breathe, and push on. The *Coffeehouse Investor's Ground Rules* will guide you to a life of wealth and happiness over the next two decades and beyond, as Bill's first book did for its readers.

I encourage you to grab your fresh-brewed coffee and enjoy Bill's thoughtful musings on investing and life. I have seen the impact these timeless Ground Rules have had on the lives of clients at Buckingham Strategic Wealth. They will have the same impact on yours.

As you embrace the Ground Rules, Bill and I invite you to share them with others. Together, we will continue to change the world, one investor at a time.

Larry Swedroe, Chief Research Officer
of Buckingham Strategic Wealth
and Buckingham Strategic Partners

Preface

I grew up on a farm, and I like telling stories about growing up on the farm. The things I learned on the farm have stuck with me throughout my life. It is the wisdom I share with you. I didn't grow up in the depression, but my grandparents did. They raised my mother and father in the depression, and I think that had something to do with how my grandparents managed their money. They didn't have online banking accounts. They didn't have mobile apps to buy and sell stocks. They didn't have a subscription to Morningstar to track mutual funds, and they didn't watch Jim Cramer on CNBC because they didn't have a television. They had a passbook savings account. This little ledger was the size of a passport, issued to them by the local bank, and they kept track of how much they saved and how much they spent, down to the penny. I know, because I have those passbooks in my possession as a keepsake of the memory of how money flowed through their life.

One grandpa was a farmer. My other grandpa was a banker. Maybe that had something to do with the meticulous financial records I kept in my own passbook savings account of the pigs I raised and sold, and the money I earned that was deposited into the bank at a savings rate much higher than the savings rates of today. That passbook savings account was our financial planning calculator. Life was simple back then, but it wasn't easy.

Everything changed in 1982. That was the year passbook savings accounts became passé.

That was the year I graduated from college and became a stock-broker. That was the year company-sponsored 401(k) plans were introduced to the workplace. That was the year the stock market started its 18-year bull market run, producing double-digit returns almost twice its historical average.

An almost unimaginable 18-year bull market run, combined with thousands and then millions of investors saving for retirement in workplace retirement plans, caused a monumental shift in our society away from a "passbook-savings mentality" of building wealth and toward a "stock-picking mentality" of building wealth.

It couldn't last forever, and it didn't. Everything came crashing down during the bear market of 1999–2002, when the S&P 500 index declined 47 percent over a three-year period and the tech-heavy NASDAQ index plummeted 78 percent from its highs. Investors who were building retirement plans on the backs of these high-flying stocks had their dreams shattered. Fortunately for them, a better way of building wealth was emerging.

Throughout the 20 years leading up to the dot-com bubble, an unconventional investment strategy was beginning to unfold. Led by Burton Malkiel's book *A Random Walk Down Wall Street*, and John Bogle's efforts at Vanguard, the simple concept of buying all the companies in a low-cost index fund was taking hold.

As luck would have it, 1998 was the year I introduced my book *The Coffeehouse Investor* to the world. Based on three timeless financial principles, its message was simple and profound – principles that form the Coffeehouse ground rules today: Save, Invest, and create a financial Plan for your future.

Soon after my book was published, I began writing a weekly investment column in The King County Journal; at that time Washington's third largest daily newspaper.

When I began writing the column, I needed to get creative in describing a Coffeehouse Investor-type portfolio to the reader, and so I designed a 60/40 portfolio of Vanguard Index Funds that looked like this.

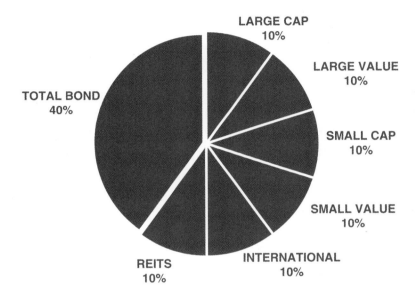

It seemed like every other week I reminded readers that my 60/40 portfolio *was just one example* of a Coffeehouse Investor-type portfolio, but I guess you cannot stop a good thing. My seven-fund portfolio took on a life of its own with investors across the nation, highlighted early on by Paul Farrell and his Lazy Portfolios at www.marketwatch.com.

The merits of this portfolio is still endorsed by "Slice & Dice" advocates and its return, going back to 1999, is closely monitored in the "Madsinger Monthly Report" at www.bogleheads.org.

Despite its enduring popularity, the portfolio's benefit isn't found in its specific construction nor its 20-year returns. It is found in investors "capturing their fair share of market returns" over time, as Mr. Bogle was fond of saying.

Since then, I have witnessed the life-changing impact of these ground rules on the lives of investors across the nation and around the world. Slowly, investors started turning away from a "picking stocks" mentality and returned to the "passbook savings account" mentality of building wealth.

The Coffeehouse Investor movement is part of a larger movement to embrace low-cost index funds as the preferred method of owning common stocks.

But the movement is much larger than index funds, because index funds and target-date funds are not some magical investment that secures your financial independence in retirement. These funds are simply building blocks within your portfolio that allow you to focus on what matters within your financial plan. The larger movement taking hold across our nation is a more meaningful vision of wealth and happiness.

For better or worse, we live in a society that has come to define wealth and happiness as an accumulation of "more" material things. Our empty pursuit of more is a byproduct of a capitalistic focus on bigger and better. In working closely with Coffeehouse Investors over the past 20 years as a financial advisor located just outside Seattle, Washington, these sages have redefined this pursuit of "more": more community, more creativity, more family, more sustainability, more equality, more of all those things that give you life, and nudge the global community forward.

That is what the ground rules are all about. We invite you to join us as we live our lives of wealth and happiness and share it with others. This book will show you how.

1

Two Lives Become One

Hello Bill,
I enjoyed attending your webinar the other night. While the information wasn't new to someone who has been a devout Coffeehouse Investor for six years already, it's always good to review the material. I believe so strongly in the Coffeehouse's philosophy that I've bought many copies of your book to give away. Right now there are many family members and friends' family members who are graduating from college. Each one receives a copy of your book and a check to get started from my wife and I. Wish I had been given such advice and a check to start with when I was their age.
Gene

For the past 20 years, Coffeehouse Investors like Gene have taken it upon themselves to change the world.

One investor at a time.

I never met Gene, but he sent me this e-mail about 10 years ago. Together, we have redefined the ground rules of investing by using low-cost index funds as building blocks for our portfolios. His e-mail is a reminder that all of us have an opportunity to touch peoples' lives in a profound way.

Now, the Energy of the Universe is asking us to do more. It is time to redefine the ground rules for a life of wealth and happiness.

- Save
- Invest
- Plan

We are asked to share these simple ground rules to nudge the global community forward and stay in sync with the unfolding universe. That is what Coffeehouse Investors are all about: taking control of your financial destiny to get on track, stay on track, and make a difference in the world.

Imagine what you could do with your life if your financial resources created harmony – not anxiety – in your pursuit of wealth and happiness. The world needs you to live your rich life, more than ever before.

When I look back over the past 20 years, Tony stands out as one example of someone who lives a life of wealth and happiness. I have watched Tony's life unfold, partly because his father, a cousin of mine, has kept me in the loop. Tony didn't pursue a career in home construction, like his father, nor a job in banking, like his grandfather. Inspired by his mother, he decided on a career in education. He wanted to teach, but he wanted *more*. He decided to broaden his reach and become a principal. Now he wants to broaden his reach even *more* and is working on his doctorate in one of the most challenging school districts in Washington State.

We will explore society's pursuit of "more" in Chapter 8, but for Tony, his pursuit of "more" nudges the global community in the right direction. Somewhere along the way, he and his wife Katie arrived at a harmony between saving for tomorrow and living their rich life today. Along the way, he was introduced to the Coffeehouse investment philosophy, and they slowed down their lives enough to make sure they are on track, allowing themselves the freedom to move forward in life, doing what they do best – raising children, teaching children, and touching lives.

Tony would probably say, "If *I* can do it, anyone can do it." It's all about the ground rules. Save. Invest. Plan. Tony's story is not exceptional, and that is what being a Coffeehouse Investor is all about – ordinary people living extraordinary lives and making a difference. An essential part of Tony's journey – an essential part of *all* our journeys – is finding the elusive harmony between planning for tomorrow and living a life of wealth and happiness today.

Behind Tony's easy-going smile is a knack for tuning in to the Energy of the Universe. I admire that; there was a time in my life when I wish I had done the same.

When I graduated from college in 1982, I was pulled in two different directions – wanting to pursue my own interest in computers and wanting a relationship with my father. I grew up in a small farming community in eastern Washington, and, like most boys, I just wanted to connect with my father. Even though I was fascinated with this new thing called a personal computer, my father loved following the stock market, and so I chose a career that fascinated my father instead of pursuing my own interest in computers.

After college, I moved to Seattle to begin my career as a stockbroker for the Wall Street firm Smith Barney. I set a goal for myself of making 100 cold calls a day, trying to capture clients and generate commissions for the firm.

It was a tough job making 100 cold calls every day, dealing with the rejection, and then doing it again the next day, and the day after that. I thought it would get easier over time, and I would become immune to the rejection as I built up my clients, but it only got worse. I felt empty emotionally and, every day, on that long walk from the bus stop to the office in downtown Seattle, my heart was telling me I needed a change.

It would be easy to look back and say that it was a mistake to pursue a Wall Street career, and stick with it as long as I did, but now it seems it was meant to be.

I hated cold calling the most. The cold-calling experts told us if we persevered through 95 rejections to gain 5 potential clients, it was a success, and to some stockbrokers, it was a formula for success. Not me. Early on, I turned away from the cold-calling and did what a lot of college graduates do when they are trying to figure things out. I called Mom.

In her infinite wisdom, she said . . .

"Get involved."

And so I did. I volunteered to coach a boys' youth basketball team. And then I volunteered to coach a girls' volleyball team.

I signed up to answer phones on the Seattle crisis line. I joined a neighborhood baseball team. I served food at homeless shelters. I signed up for a mountaineering class and then a cooking class.

Even though I was miserable at work, I found meaning in those activities. I fell in love with the mountains, the water, and, most of all, the people of Seattle, but I still hated cold-calling. Selling stocks was a commission-driven business, and the idea of helping clients reach their financial goals never registered with the management of the brokerage firm.

Although I was a failure at selling stocks, I discovered I was good at getting clients to buy bonds. In the early 1980s, the people I was calling in the wealthy neighborhoods of Seattle didn't want stocks; they wanted AA-rated tax-free bonds with great yields – and back then, they *were* great yields. My cold-calling script went something like this . . .

> *Hi, this is Bill from Smith Barney. The State of Washington is issuing a AA-rated tax-free bond next week with a great yield on it, do you want any?*

These people didn't care if I was a Bill, Bob, or Brian. All they heard was

- Smith Barney
- State of Washington
- AA-rated
- Great yield

When I finished calling the wealthy neighborhoods of Seattle, I called the wealthy neighborhoods of Portland, Oregon, where my pitch worked just as well.

- Smith Barney
- State of Oregon
- AA-rated
- Great yield

These investors didn't want the risk of stocks. They wanted a secure stream of income.

I eventually had clients in several states across the nation, was making a good living as one of Smith Barney's largest municipal bond brokers, but I still had that empty feeling inside. Looking back, that emptiness was simply the Energy of the Universe nudging me to pursue a richer life. I had no idea what was in store for me, but after 10 years of selling bonds, I had to make a change.

My decision to quit my job was prompted by a discussion I had with the dad of one of my volleyball players. As the executive director of Hospice of Seattle, he invited me to serve on the hospice community advisory board. I also worked as a hospice volunteer, connecting with residents, listening to their stories, and holding their hands.

Looking back, that experience of holding hands and listening to stories allowed me to embrace my own mortality. The wisdom of Confucius sums up the emotions I felt in meeting with hospice residents.

> *A man has two lives to live, and the second one begins when he realizes he only has one.*

The more time I spent connecting with hospice residents, the more I came to grips with my one life to live. I needed to make a change, and that was the motivation to end my career at Smith Barney.

I knew it was the right decision, but it was still an empty feeling, stepping away from a job in finance with nothing in front of me to pursue. I felt like I had wasted 10 years of my life. It didn't help that I had three brothers and four sisters who were raising families and doing great things with their lives. That made me feel even more lost, and so I packed my bags and moved 70 miles north of Seattle, to a little town called La Conner. In that little town I had the same feelings of isolation and confusion I endured when I first moved to Seattle, but this time I had a game plan.

I got involved.

I climbed mountains; I volunteered at a hospital; I took classes and taught classes, while contemplating my next steps. I signed up for the two-day Seattle to Portland (STP) bike ride, and after a long first day of biking, at the halfway point, our biking crew spent the night at a Jesuit retreat house. Late in the evening, I had a conversation with Alexis, a spiritual counselor. When I shared my emptiness with her, she gently responded, "When you return to La Conner, go dig in the dirt, and you will figure it out."

After I returned to La Conner, I planted a garden, and then tended my rose bushes for the next two years while living off the small savings I had accumulated during my years at Smith Barney.

It wasn't an instant epiphany, but while digging in the dirt, planting my garden, and tending the rose bushes, I figured it out. A radical movement was taking hold across the investing landscape, spurred on by Burton Malkiel's book *A Random Walk Down Wall Street* and John Bogle's work at Vanguard.

The core idea of this movement was elegant in its simplicity. Instead of searching out the top companies for a successful investing experience, the best way to maximize your returns in the stock market was to own all the companies through a low-cost index fund.

I wanted to participate in this radical movement. I was convinced it would have a meaningful impact on the lives of investors by allowing them to turn their attention away from the daily gyrations of the stock market and toward some simple ground rules in pursuit of wealth and happiness.

- Save
- Invest
- Plan

I also knew this radical idea would require a new way of thinking for many investors, including me. When you are around a father for 22 years who is obsessed with picking stocks, and then get involved in an industry for the next 10 years that is obsessed with picking stocks, well, you just kind of take it for granted that the best way to invest in the stock market is picking the top stocks.

The more I thought about this movement, the more I realized I had discovered my purpose in life. Today, index funds have captured the attention of investors around the world, but in 1993 most investors had no idea what an index fund was.

I read what seemed like the only two books on index funds, by Burton Malkiel and John Bogle, but I knew my brothers and sisters probably would not read those books. Like most investors who are saving and investing money for retirement, they are too busy with their lives to read a finance book.

That was the opportunity I was looking for. I wanted to write a book for investors like Gene, Tony, and my seven brothers and sisters – people who are pursuing wealth and happiness – not on Wall Street's terms, but on their own.

I spent the next couple of years writing the manuscript and searching out publishers, finally submitting my completed draft to 28 publishing companies.

Every publishing company rejected it. With each visit to the mailbox, and each rejection letter, I was thinking to myself, "This is harder than I thought."

I figured if I was persistent enough, I would eventually find a publisher for my book, and so I headed back to the bookstore, purchased the *1996 Guide to Literary Agents*, and started all over. This time I sent query letters and sample chapters to 46 literary agents, intent on finding someone who would help me find someone to publish my simple little book.

The rejection letters kept coming. Looking back on my persistence at getting published amid all those rejections, the rejections I dealt with making all those cold calls at Smith Barney steeled me to push on. Even though I was now getting rejected by publishers and literary agents, I was inspired because at least I was pursuing my dream. I was tuned in to the Energy of the Universe. Then one day, I got an acceptance letter. An agent in New York wanted to represent my manuscript and within a few months he secured a book deal for me.

After four years of trying and failing, I finally had a book contract in hand that called for delivery of a 60,000 word manuscript, and went to work re-writing sections of the book based on discussions with Suzanne, my new editor at the publishing company.

When my revised manuscript was completed, I had a big problem. Everything I needed to say to get my point across was said in 35,000 words. I had 25,000 words to go to get to 60,000.

The contract didn't say specifically what the 60,000 words had to be about, and so I started writing stories, not about the financial markets, but about my life. I wrote about growing up on a wheat farm on the banks of the Snake River in the Southeastern corner of the state of Washington. I wrote about my mountain climbing experiences in the Northwest and Alaska. I wrote about anything I could think of so that I could submit a manuscript of 60,000 words.

When it came time to edit the book, I flew down to Atlanta, Georgia, to meet with Suzanne – the same weekend an earlier book she edited, *The Millionaire Next Door*, reached no. 1 on the *New York Times* bestseller list.

When Suzanne started editing my book, she began by eliminating lots of charts and statistics from my manuscript and keeping all my personal stories that I had included to fill up the book. I told her, "Hey, Suzanne, you are taking out all the good stuff. I need that data to prove my point." She replied with wisdom I will never forget. "Bill, investing isn't about charts and statistics, it is about reaching a harmony with your money in the way you live your life."

Who am I to argue with the editor of a *New York Times* bestseller?

As *The Coffeehouse Investor* was about to go to press, Suzanne and I combed over the book, looking for mistakes. This anxiety was driven in part by another recently published personal finance book, *The Beardstown Ladies*, written by a group of women who supposedly had generated great returns from their investment club's stock-picking prowess. Unfortunately, these ladies had made a mistake in the way they calculated their returns. It turns out their stock selections didn't perform anywhere near what was promoted in the book. I suspect it was an honest mistake but an embarrassing one, and Suzanne was not about to be embarrassed by one of her books. We went over the manuscript again and again, and finally the book went to print.

Soon after *The Coffeehouse Investor* hit the bookstores we started receiving e-mail from investors across the country, pointing out a glaring mistake. I had written a chapter on the significant impact of dividend reinvestment on a portfolio's total return, titled, "My Favorite Piece of Pie." At the end of the chapter I included a pumpkin pie recipe, but I had left out the sugar. Readers were quick to point out this mistake, and even sent me their grandmas' favorite pumpkin pie recipes.

- Save
- Invest
- Plan

Over the years I have received lots of e-mail from readers expressing an appreciation for a book short on charts and statistics, but long on how to build wealth, ignore Wall Street, and get on with their lives.

One e-mail from a young woman said that her mother had a unique and successful investing approach. She bought all the stocks that her father sold, because after he sold them, they inevitably went up.

I received another e-mail from a woman who said that she was rethinking the firing of her stockbroker, because she now had no one to yell at when her stocks declined in value.

Of all the e-mail I received, my favorite was from a Californian named David who wrote the following:

> *Balance in Life, Balance in Family, Balance in Investing. I have finally found an investment philosophy that preaches what I have felt my entire life. I am a lucky man as I approach retirement. I have three healthy children, I am more in love with my wife than ever before, and I have made a few modest, but wise investments along the way. I wonder how many 55-year-old elementary school principals can say the same. Your approach seems a perfect fit for everyone as investing for our retirements becomes more and more important in our society.*

David was right. Investing for retirement has become more and more important, and we'll talk about this later in the book. The thing I liked most about David's e-mail was that he said the Coffeehouse Investor philosophy was something he had *felt his entire life*. I wasn't sharing an investment club's secret formula for picking stocks. I wasn't telling him anything he didn't already know. David was simply embracing the Coffeehouse ground rules.

- Save
- Invest
- Plan

Getting a book published was just the beginning of my Coffeehouse journey.

It was up to me to get readers to buy the book. I needed to do some promoting, so I started reaching out to local and national media outlets to publicize the book.

That was harder than I thought, but, hey, I'm used to rejection.

It was early 1999, when the novelty of online trading accounts converged with the hot stocks of the dot-com boom. It seemed like every investor, except me, was getting rich overnight. There wasn't much interest in a book on the wisdom of buying index funds and building wealth slowly when you could sit at your computer, trade stocks in your pajamas, and get rich overnight.

I was tuned in to the Energy of the Universe, and the Energy of the Universe was smiling back, introducing me to a few investors who did take notice.

I figured, why not call a few coffeehouses, and see if they might be interested in my book? Turns out the book buyer for Starbucks liked it, and placed an order for 8,000 books. A fellow board member of Hospice of Seattle read my book, liked it, and introduced me to the business editor of Washington's third largest daily newspaper, in the heart of Boeing and Microsoft country. I reached out and asked the editor if he would be open to writing a book review of *The Coffeehouse Investor*.

He liked it, and suggested that I write the book review myself. So I did. After submitting it, I offered a follow-up column the next week, and he agreed to that. I ended up writing a column, "The Coffeehouse Investor," in that paper for eight years, and said the same thing each week:

- Save
- Invest
- Plan

As a reader once responded to me, "Repetition doesn't just work in rock 'n' roll."

I started the column in 1999, about the same time the stock market, fueled by the dot-com boom, reached its pinnacle, and then started its three-year slide. The "pajama crowd" had to go back to work.

I didn't get paid to write the weekly column, but the business editor allowed me to promote a seminar to be held at the local library, and so I did, holding my breath to see if anyone would show up.

It was packed.

It was packed with people who were nervous about their declining portfolios. It was packed with people who were trying to sort out this concept of getting rich in pajamas with a deeper longing to live a life of wealth and happiness.

It was packed with people who intuitively understood the logic of owning index funds and wanted to incorporate the Coffeehouse ground rules into their portfolios and, more importantly, into their lives.

I had left a world of Wall Street that was consumed with picking stocks and generating commissions. The Energy of the Universe, through a weekly column in the local newspaper, allowed me to enter the world of financial planning as a co-owner of a Registered Investment Advisor (RIA) firm to help others reach their financial goals.

A favorite Coffeehouse Investor was a woman I'll call Carol, who connected with the ground rules. She felt out of control with her finances, having lost a significant portion of her portfolio over the previous six months from the dot-com crash. With retirement on the horizon, she wanted to make some changes. She wanted to get on track and stay on track.

First, we figured out what her monthly expenses would be in retirement. Next, we calculated how much she needed to save each month over the next 10 years to cover her burn rate in retirement. I remember that discussion, because what Carol needed to save was about the same amount she was already saving in her workplace retirement plan. Like many of you, Carol was already on track, but needed confirmation to stay on track. At that moment she realized that she, not Wall Street, was in control of her financial destiny.

Carol's story is important for a couple of reasons. First, she didn't have any interest in following the stock market, which allowed her to focus on her saving, and more importantly, her life. Second, she retired one year before the big stock market drop in 2008, and didn't need to return to work. Why? Because bear markets are part of life, and when you build a bear market into your financial plan and asset allocation decision, you can endure bear markets, if not enjoy them. Carol was emotionally and financially prepared for bear markets, as we all should be.

Now, in retirement, she focuses on her spending, not on Wall Street, which allows her to be in control of the drawdown of her portfolio. Carol lives a rich life in retirement because she, not Wall Street, is in control of her financial destiny.

Carol knows that an integral part of finding harmony within a financial plan is knowing you are on track and ignoring Wall Street. But ignoring Wall Street does not mean ignoring what is going on in the world. That is impossible.

How can you ignore the dot-com meltdown and the 9/11 terrorist attack?

How can you ignore the financial crisis of 2008?

How can you ignore the COVID-19 pandemic of 2020?

You can't ignore world events. You shouldn't. It is life. But you do have the power to control the things that are in your control, like the Coffeehouse ground rules. You have the power to control how many times you look at your portfolio throughout the year. You have the power to keep track of your spending. Most of all, you have the power to turn your attention toward your essential creativity to discover a purpose in life that is more life-giving than the daily commotion of Wall Street.

If you are in search of the same energy for life that Carol possesses, it might be the right time for you to turn away from Wall Street, dig in the dirt, and discover your rich life that awaits you.

That is what being a Coffeehouse Investor is all about.

We are at a point of transition. As the world moves forward from a focus on survival of the fittest to sustainability for all, it will challenge us to use our essential creativity and shared wisdom to address problems from new dimensions, new structures, new concepts, and maybe even reinvent ourselves along the way.

Deep inside, we are moved to share our wisdom with the global community to make it a better place. It is this great Energy of the Universe that drives communities, cultures, companies, countries, and, yes, even stock markets, to new heights. The more you can put your good energy into this great unfolding, the better off we all will be.

We owe it to each other to make this a better world.

You owe it to yourself to live a life you richly deserve. It's time to discuss the ground rules.

2

Ground Rule 1: Save

In the big picture of life, saving for retirement is a relatively new concept. It isn't a tradition that has been passed down through generations. Socking money away for 25 years of unemployment just isn't built into our saving DNA. If you are trying to figure it out, you are not alone.

There is a popular notion that Americans are not good at saving, especially for retirement; that they just want to live in the moment and spend money on what makes them happy today.

That may be true for some, but not for you. You know that finding a harmony between how much you save for the future and how you spend your money today is in your own hands.

It is up to you to make it happen, even though trying to calculate how much to save today for 25 years of unemployment can be so daunting that you hardly know where to start. Over the past 20 years, Coffeehouse Investors have revealed that the best place to start is at the very beginning – with a vision of what you want.

Take a moment and reflect on a time in your life when you had a vision of saving up for something, and you reached that goal. That is the same sense of purpose you need now, and the benefit transcends reaching that saving goal sometime down the road. There is an equally important benefit of knowing you are on track today.

For me, my vision was saving for a $15 mitt. I made it happen and that $15 saving experience sticks with me to this day when I am tempted to tinker around with my portfolio instead of refocusing my attention on what matters to stay on track.

Your vision may change over time, and that is all right; it is called life. It simply requires some adjustments in your financial plan to stay on track. We will review your ever-changing financial plan later in Chapter 6.

If you are a 25-year-old and just starting to save, "getting on track" might mean socking away 15 percent of your salary in a workplace retirement plan. If you are 55 years old and just starting to save, "on track" takes on a new meaning, but it's never too late to start getting on track.

As we go through life, each of us has different spending and saving goals. I might want to play golf on the weekends and you might want to go camping. I might want to vacation on the glaciers of Mt. Rainier, while you prefer the beaches of Hawaii. When it comes to saving for retirement, however, most of us want the same thing: a lifestyle that reflects the one we hoped for while we were working.

Now, about that $15 mitt. When I look at saving in my own life, I remember the rope that hung from the ceiling of an old farm shed. At the end of the rope was a baseball about 3 feet above the ground; that was how my brother and I learned to hit a baseball.

Put me in coach, I'm ready to play.

In another corner of the shed cyanide tablets were stored up to get rid of coyotes that circled the farm at night. We had only one ground rule when playing baseball in that shed – stay away from the cyanide tablets. I spent hours hitting that baseball with my younger brother, avoiding the cyanide tablets, and daydreaming of big things to come.

By the time I was five, my daydream took me to Boston because Ted Williams had played for the Red Sox and he was my father's favorite player. On my fifth birthday I got a flimsy little mitt, and when I wasn't hitting, I was catching fly balls in the outfield.

Look at me, I can be, centerfield.

Luckily our farmhouse had a steeply pitched roof that allowed me to throw the baseball up on the roof, and as it rolled back down, I wasn't a kid on the farm; I was a center fielder in Fenway Park, positioned to catch the last out of the World Series.

One summer evening my father took my brother and me to see the real thing. We picked up a bunch of cousins in our Chevrolet station wagon and drove 18 miles to Lewiston, Idaho, to watch the Lewis-Clark Broncs, the Oakland A's farm team, play baseball. They had a center fielder named Reggie Jackson, and boy, could he play ball.

My daydreams of the big leagues took on a whole new meaning after watching Reggie Jackson play baseball. Making it to the big leagues was a distant dream. But playing ball for the Lewis-Clark Broncs in Lewiston, Idaho, was something I could relate to, because Lewiston was right down the hill, the city where I brought my pigs to market. I could handle that.

By the third grade I was old enough to try out for Little League, but I had a big problem: I needed a new mitt. When you are a kid playing ball you pay close attention to the size of the other kids' mitts, and I especially noticed Brian's mitt. To me, his mitt looked bigger than Reggie Jackson's mitt, and I spotted it every time we played baseball at recess at Guardian Angel School.

The thought of showing up for Little League tryouts with a flimsy little mitt gnawed at me and kept me awake at night. The tryouts were three months away, so I told my father I needed a new mitt. Like most fathers of that era, except maybe Brian's dad, he wasn't going to just buy me a new mitt. I had to earn it.

And so, in addition to my chores of chopping thistles, mowing lawns, feeding pigs, and cleaning out the barn, I earned extra money for the mitt by weeding the test plots on our farm, planted by the wheat breeders of Washington State University.

I was obsessed with getting that mitt. I knew which mitt I wanted and how much it cost. I knew how many days it was to the Little League tryouts. I figured out that if I could weed the test plots an hour a day, five days a week, for three months at 25 cents an hour, I'd have enough money to buy that mitt.

It was an exhilarating feeling to be in complete control of my financial destiny. I didn't have to rely on Santa and I especially didn't have to rely on my father. When I was weeding those test plots, I wasn't thinking about Little League tryouts, I was daydreaming about playing center field for the Lewis-Clark Broncs.

Every night after weeding, before I fell asleep, I would recalculate how many hours of weeding I had left before the tryouts, so it matched up with how much more I needed to buy that mitt. I made sure I was on track.

I still have that $15 mitt. And I still have the flimsy mitt it replaced. Today, whenever I start to think of bad weather and bear markets, I remember those mitts and remind myself that I am in control of my financial destiny.

Wall Streeters might think there is a big difference between working three months to save up for a mitt and working four decades to save up for retirement. After connecting with Coffeehouse Investors over the past 20 years, I respectfully disagree. You have revealed it is the same as saving for a $15 mitt. You have got to save. It is the first ground rule of a life of wealth and happiness.

I'm the first to admit that saving for retirement can be a bit more complicated than saving up for a mitt when you have to sort through things like 401(k) accounts, Roth 401(k) accounts, individual retirement accounts, Roth IRA accounts, non-deductible IRA accounts, and more. But the ground rule never changes.

You've got to save.

For some, the challenge to save enough becomes overwhelming because Wall Street shows up and wants to divert your attention from saving to things that are out of your control, like

- Sector funds
- Structured notes
- Recessions
- 4 percent rules
- Correlation coefficients
- Standard deviations
- Monte Carlo simulations
- Efficient frontiers
- Sharpe ratios
- CAPM
- Alternatives
- Bitcoin

just to name a few.

You can label this financial jargon however you like, and, of course, this stuff is important to Wall Street and Academia. However, I suspect this stuff was not very important to the characters in *The Millionaire Next Door*. I know it was irrelevant to my municipal bond clients at Smith Barney. I know it was irrelevant to my grandparents. After 20 years I know it is irrelevant to Coffeehouse Investors.

The problem with dealing with Wall Street, when trying to answer, "Am I on track?" is that Wall Street jargon distracts you from exploring the emotions of your heart, and how you create a harmony with the money that flows through your life.

In order to explore those emotions with you, Wall Street and Academia would have to stop talking and start listening, and that will never happen because, as we will discover in the next chapter, Wall Street thinks they are smarter than you. It is much easier for them to discuss Monte Carlo simulations, structured notes, and Sharpe ratios than it is to listen to your emotions about saving up for a $15 mitt.

Are we on track? That was the question Cathy and Dan had when they called me in January 2019, with the stock market starting to recover from a steep December decline. A few minutes into the call, I sensed that, like many Americans, they were not on track.

Cathy was concerned that her 401(k) balance had plummeted 20 percent in December. Dan was concerned about the outlook for the sector funds he had chosen in his trading account.

They had small accounts all over the place including old IRAs, old 401(k)s, and current 401(k)s. I suggested they consolidate their accounts, build a simple Coffeehouse Investor portfolio, and focus less on the markets and more on their saving.

One year and two months later, when the COVID-19 pandemic caused the stock market to plummet 30 percent, Cathy and Dan called me back with the same anxieties. Cathy was concerned that her 401(k) balance had plummeted about 30 percent. Dan was still concerned about the outlook for the sector funds in his trading account.

When I prodded a little more, they admitted they hadn't done a thing since we had spoken on the phone over a year ago.

It was time to discuss the ground rules.

I asked them what their retirement goals were, and how much they expected to spend each month in retirement. They didn't have much to say, preferring instead to talk about falling stock markets and sector funds.

I politely asked them to stop talking about Wall Street for a moment and talk about themselves. That is when they discovered the ground rules, and that is when they started to get on track.

I suggested they create a vision of retiring at 70, with a lifestyle similar to the one they are living today.

I pressed them on their current monthly burn rate (expenses), and they confessed that they didn't keep track of their expenses, although they estimated that it was close to $7,000. Next, after a little digging, they discovered that their combined Social Security payments at age 70 would be about $5,000. We determined that they needed to save up enough money over the next 10 years to cover the $2,000 monthly shortfall in retirement.

They are not buying a $15 mitt here, but there was nothing too complicated about coming up with these numbers.

When Cathy and Dan discovered how much they needed to save each month to cover that monthly shortfall in retirement, they responded, "We can do that!" The excitement in their voices revealed my same emotions when I devised a game plan to buy that mitt.

"We can do that!" is an essential first step in turning away from Wall Street and creating harmony with how money flows through your life – recognizing that you have it in you to get on track and stay on track.

Other things will come up in Cathy and Dan's life over the next 10 years requiring adjustments to their financial plan, and that's okay. At least they are beginning a conversation to create financial harmony on their own terms.

I told Cathy and Dan something I discovered long ago. It is a lot easier to save if you don't have to think about saving. While Cathy's workplace retirement plan had an automatic payroll deduction, Dan was self-employed and needed to establish his own monthly automatic deduction plan from the family checking account.

With all the technology created by Wall Street to help analyze your portfolio, the best wealth-building technology ever created is still the automatic transfer of funds into a retirement account.

I encouraged Cathy and Dan to keep track of their expenses throughout the year – not down to the penny, but enough so that they have a good idea of how money flows through their lives – an essential component to getting on track and staying on track. This awareness has benefits far beyond getting on track – it allows you to redirect the flow of money toward components of your life that foster a life of wealth and happiness. The simple act of tracking expenses could change their lives forever. I know it changed mine.

I started keeping track of my expenses at a time in my life when I was forced to keep track. It was a matter of survival. For the first time, I became aware of how money flowed through my life.

When I quit my job as a stockbroker and moved to La Conner to figure things out, my earnings went to zero. Although I had saved up a few dollars, I crunched the numbers just as I did when creating a plan to buy that $15 mitt. I figured I could spend $700 a month for two years before I had to go back to work. With rent costing me $300 I became keenly aware of how I spent the remaining $400. I knew I wouldn't be eating those fancy dinners I had grown accustomed to as a stockbroker at Smith Barney.

Keeping track provided something far greater than making sure I kept my monthly burn rate under $700. It challenged me to review my spending on empty consumption, and redirect those dollars to accentuate my creativity.

Empty spending had snuck into my life as a stockbroker when my earnings outpaced the dollars I needed for the essentials of food, healthcare, and shelter.

While I was working, my DNA of wanting more stuff outweighed my DNA of saving for retirement.

When I wasn't working, I still wanted "more," which meant I needed to pursue a different type of "more," like more creativity, more community, more exploration of what I wanted to share with the world, more discovery of me.

That might be your challenge as well, as you create a harmony with money your life. Take time to discover the "more" in your life that gives meaning to your life. Today, I am back at work, and I still need to deal with the emotions of wanting "more," so it remains a healthy part of my DNA for the rest of my life.

When I moved to La Conner, I was faced with the opportunity to turn my monthly $700 scarcity mentality into a $700 abundance mentality. It didn't happen overnight, but my essential creativity kicked in soon enough.

Although I was no longer spending $50 on fancy dinners, I still had to eat. So I pulled out the hand-crank pasta machine I had picked up in Italy 10 years earlier, and improved on my pasta-making skills. I rediscovered the feeling of mixing flour and eggs with my hands and turning it into dough that I hand-cranked into fettuccine noodles.

During the day I worked on *The Coffeehouse Investor*, and at night I made pasta. The next day I worked on *The Coffeehouse Investor* and at night I made pasta. I was having so much fun working on *The Coffeehouse Investor* and making pasta that I started teaching investment classes and pasta-making classes at Northwest Freedom University in Bellingham, Washington. The investment class was made up mostly of women, and the pasta class was filled up mostly with men. At the end of four weeks, the women from the investment class started showing up at the pasta-making class and I was having the time of my life.

Twenty-five years ago, I slowed my life down enough to review and create harmony with the flow of money in my life. Today, I still perform the same review, and I invite you to do the same. If you think that what I did 25 years ago, keeping track of how I spent my $700, has no relation to your life today of paying a mortgage, raising children, and living your busy life, you are right.

But the ground rules never change.

You want to live a rich life today while making sure that you are on track for retirement tomorrow. Your rich life today is determined by how you focus on your creativity, not consumption. It requires an honest assessment of how you are spending your dollars, and then directing those dollars towards your essential creativity and your retirement.

There is a movement afoot called FIRE (Financial Independence Retire Early), of people who are slowing down to review and redirect the flow of money to create a better harmony in their lives. Many who engage in FIRE are intent on saving a sizable amount of their salary to create financial independence and the possibility of early retirement.

This movement has garnered its share of criticism, ranging from "Why would anyone want to live such a Spartan lifestyle today?" to "Why would anyone want to retire at 40?" But hey, if someone wants to save 80 percent of their salary by making pasta every night so they can retire early and enjoy those tulip fields in La Conner the rest of their life, who am I to argue otherwise?

If someone wants to retire early, and maps out a game plan to accomplish that, good for them. What fascinates me is not the RE part of the FIRE movement, but the FI part – the conscious effort to take a hard look at your expenses and redirect most of those dollars to establishing financial independence – living life on your own terms.

The people focusing on FIRE are doing what we *all* should do – conduct a critical review of how money flows through our life. At the very least, the awareness of how you spend your money allows you the opportunity to have a meaningful conversation with yourself, and maybe your partner, to explore whether the way you spend money is truly aligned with how you want to live your life. That is the greatest benefit of keeping track.

Awareness of how money flows in your life is not a new-age millennial thing. For many, in years past, it was an exercise in survival.

My grandparents came from different corners of the nation. One set of grandparents raised a family on the banks of the Snake River. The other set of grandparents raised a family in Santa Monica, California, in the shadow of Hollywood, before moving to Spokane, Washington. Both sets of grandparents had at least two things in common: they raised their families through the Great Depression and they kept a detailed ledger on how they spent their money – ledgers that are now on my bookshelf as a reminder of what is important to me in building a life of wealth and happiness.

Their harmony with money was built with the financial awareness of those in the FIRE movement. It is the same focus Coffeehouse Investors have embraced over the past 20 years and should be your focus as well.

Cathy and Dan started their journey to get on track by shifting their conversation away from Wall Street and beginning to focus on how money flows through their lives.

When I explored the idea of taking more time to nurture their essential creativity, Cathy and Dan revealed a daydream that had been percolating for years. They had created a small side business and were trying to launch it in their spare time. The more we talked about it, the more excited they became about their daydream.

Based on what they shared with me, over the next 10 years, this little business idea could have a meaningful impact on their financial well-being in retirement.

The way I see it, the greatest benefit of their little idea is it directs their daydreams and emotions away from Wall Street today and toward their essential creativity.

That is a life of wealth and happiness.

The harmony we create with our money allows us to live a life of abundance, not scarcity. That is the essence of the FIRE movement. They transform what some might call a scarcity mentality into a pursuit of "more" – more freedom, more independence, and more of feeling alive.

Getting on track nudges you to tune in to the Energy of the Universe, because you are in control of your financial destiny.

That's what we will explore next.

3

Women, Winning in Wealth

I'm not buying it.

Only 24 percent of women are confident in their investing skills?[1] Not in my world and not in yours. Try 100 percent. You can have this investing thing down cold because the two things that matter most are the checkbook and common sense.

---

[1] 2018 Fidelity Women and Investing Study.

In the past, you have probably listened to the other half proclaim, "I am smarter than you" in your search for investment advice. Not anymore. From here on out, the narrative is changed. You are smarter than them with your checkbook and common sense.

As Natalie, Lisa, Denise, and Tina reveal later in this chapter, whether you are 35, 23, 45, or 90, your checkbook and common sense are what count for a life of wealth and happiness.

First, meet Natalie. For the past 10 years, I have urged Natalie, a single mother of two teenagers, to establish and contribute to an IRA. Every time I connected with her, the response was always, "I don't understand the stock market and I don't want to lose money in it." I wondered, at times, if that was simply a deflection caused by life getting in the way. Like most mothers, her children came first, and only then did she take care of herself.

In 2018, Natalie reached out to me. Her workplace had a new retirement plan and she wanted to get the employer's match. I think she figured out that if she didn't start saving for retirement, there wasn't going to be anything for her to live on at retirement except Social Security. Natalie wanted more than that. She wanted to get on track.

She showed me the retirement plan's long lineup of funds, and revealed her hesitancy to ask for help. Again, she reminded me, "I don't understand the stock market and I don't want to lose money in it."

I asked if she had a rainy-day fund, and she said yes. I asked if she had created a will for the family, and her answer was no. Did she have life insurance for her girls? No. Was she saving for her daughters' college education? No. Then she smiled and said, "But I'm really good at managing my checkbook."

She smiled again, and said, "Just tell me how much I need to save, and I'll figure out a way to do it." We calculated her monthly contribution to the plan, and the impact it would have on her monthly income later in life.

She figured out a way to do it.

When it comes to personal finances, the narrative perpetuated by the financial industry and their motto, "I am smarter than you," is that women just aren't that good at managing money. My experience has been quite the opposite. Like Natalie, you hold the key to your financial destiny because you control your checkbook and have common sense.

Natalie's story should serve as inspiration for you to take what you have already mastered, the checkbook and common sense, and expand it to a broader array of financial planning topics in pursuit of wealth and happiness.

In early 2019, a report by UBS was released titled "Own Your Worth – Why Women Should Take Control of Their Wealth to Achieve Financial Well-Being."[2]

This survey of almost 3,700 married women around the world revealed that more than 80 percent of them are involved in the day-to-day decisions of household expenses. However, almost 60 percent of the women do not engage in longer-term financial planning of investing, retirement, and insurance.

---

[2]UBS. (2019). Own Your Worth: Why women should take control of their wealth to achieve financial well-being. *UBS Investor Watch – Global Insights: What's on Investors' Minds* 1.

Women know they need longer-term financial planning, but they don't carry through with it, because they don't feel confident with major money decisions.

The report cited that 68 percent of women believed they would outlive their spouses, and stated the following needs for financial planning:

- 76 percent wanted retirement planning
- 72 percent wanted long-term care planning
- 68 percent wanted insurance planning

Taking charge of your financial destiny means changing your own narrative toward investing. No one is smarter than you. The confidence you have with investing now carries over to the financial planning issues that matter.

The way I see it, Wall Street won't change. The industry will forever suggest that picking stocks, predicting trends, and forecasting economies is essential to your well-being. In doing so, they continue to promote their motto, "I am smarter than you."

Fortunately, most workplace retirement plans have evolved over the years to include investment choices that allow you to build a Coffeehouse Investor–type portfolio with one investment – a target date fund – and you don't need Wall Street's help to do that. The result? You have this investing thing down cold and can begin to discuss planning issues that matter.

Owning your retirement "down cold" is essential, because there might come a time in your life, as the survey suggests, when you *will* want additional guidance on things like retirement planning, long-term care planning, and insurance planning. Wall Street will *still* imply "I am smarter than you" by giving financial planning advice like this:

- Pick top-performing stocks
- Identify leading trends
- Predict business cycles and market cycles

Instead of reviewing the things you want to plan for, like:

- Insurance planning
- Retirement planning
- Healthcare planning
- Educational funding
- Tax planning
- Charitable giving
- Eldercare planning
- Asset location
- Asset allocation

Building a portfolio of low-cost index funds is an essential component to your life of wealth and happiness because it maximizes the returns within each basket, or asset class in your portfolio.

A far greater benefit of a Coffeehouse Investor–type portfolio is the emotional freedom it allows you to focus on financial planning issues that count.

Wall Street doesn't like the idea that you can build a Coffeehouse Investor–type portfolio without their help. They will never acknowledge that you are smarter than them because you control the checkbook and common sense.

After my career at Smith Barney, around 1995 I reconnected with a friend of mine, Joe, a senior executive in Smith Barney's mutual fund department in New York. I shared my work in creating *The Coffeehouse Investor*, and his response was a brusque, "Index funds will never catch on with investors."

Wall Street is creative in the way it discredits the idea of index funds in favor of active stock selection. Even today, amid the growing popularity of index funds, Wall Street companies continue to promote professional stockpicking for portfolio management; it goes something like this:

Why settle for average when you can beat the average?

To answer that, let's look at it from a common-sense standpoint. When investing in the stock market, you have three choices:

1. You can pick stocks yourself.
2. You can have a professional stock picker, or an actively managed mutual fund, pick stocks for you.
3. You can invest in all the stocks through a passively managed index fund.

Logically, you would think that a professional stock picker could pick enough good stocks and avoid enough bad stocks to consistently outperform the stock market average.

They can't. They don't.

Because markets are efficient, a concept we discuss in Chapter 4, well over 80 percent of actively managed funds underperformed their respective indexes, or benchmarks, over the past 10 years.[3]

---

[3]S&P Dow Jones Indices. (2019). SPIVA U.S. scorecard year-end 2019.

That doesn't stop Wall Street from continuing to profess, "I am smarter than you."

Why settle for average when you can beat the average?

In reviewing the choices with Natalie inside her workplace retirement plan, she didn't just want me to pick a few mutual funds for her. She wanted to understand the reasoning behind my suggestion.

That's who Natalie is. When it comes to investing her own money, she wants to understand her decision, because she is the one that has to live with her decisions.

Wall Street is tenacious in the way it proclaims "I am smarter than you" when it comes to picking stocks. So, when I created *The Coffeehouse Investor* more than a quarter century ago, I devised a little game called "Outfox the Box" for investors like Natalie to understand her decision *and* own her decision.

I want Natalie to make her decision not because John Bogle advocated it, not because Burton Malkiel wrote about it, not because I suggested it, but because it appeals to her common sense.

Keeping in mind that about 80 percent of actively managed funds underperformed their respective benchmarks the past ten years, my game of Outfox the Box goes like this:

There are 10 boxes and each box has from $1,000 to $10,000 in it. You know how much is in each box. Which one would you choose?

$1,000	$2,000	$3,000	$4,000	$5,000
$6,000	$7,000	$8,000	$9,000	$10,000

The obvious choice is the $10,000 box.

Then I covered up the amounts in each box, except for the box with $8,000.

Now which one will you choose?

?	?	$8,000	?	?
?	?	?	?	?

In this case, the $8,000 box is the obvious choice. It is common sense.

It *is* possible to choose the $10,000 box and beat the market, but it's not worth the risk of choosing a box with a much smaller amount.

I have presented this game of Outfox the Box numerous times to Coffeehouse Investors at seminars, webinars, and with Natalie. The response is always the same.

Natalie chose the $8,000 box. She owns the entire market. From here on out, for the rest of her life, Natalie realizes that owning top stocks has nothing to do with creating a financial plan and building a life of wealth and happiness.

For Natalie, it's all about managing her checkbook and relying on her common sense.

We discussed her concern about losing money in the stock market. I told her she *will* lose money in the stock market. There *will* be days when the stock market drops and there will be years when the stock market drops. Over a lifetime of investing, studies have shown that the stock market drops about 20 percent or more every seven years.[4] That's the stock market for you. It's two steps forward and one step back. I drew a picture for her to paste on her closet wall, to review the next time the market drops 10, 20, or 30 percent, or more. It looked like this graph:

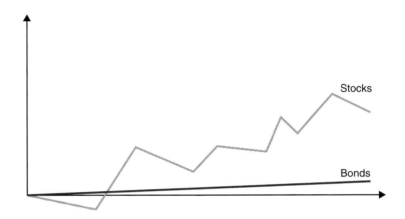

I told Natalie she had a choice of sticking all her retirement contributions in bond funds and settling for a 2 percent return, or investing some of her contributions in the stock market, living with the short-term volatility, and the expectation of higher returns over time and the opportunity for a higher monthly income when she retires. Dividing a portfolio between stocks and bonds, also known as your asset allocation, will be reviewed in Chapter 6.

It is easy to see the benefits of the stock market's expected higher returns over time when you see it on a piece of paper. We don't live on a piece of paper. We live in the moment, and that moment can include stock market declines that can last several years.

_____

[4]Source: Capital Group

In the moment, it wasn't easy to look beyond the dot-com bust and terrorist attack of 9/11. In the moment, it wasn't easy to look beyond the financial crisis of 2008. In the moment, it isn't easy to look beyond the COVID-19 pandemic with a conviction that better days are ahead for our global community.

It won't be easy to live in the moment during the next bear market. Natalie knows that control of the checkbook and common sense will see her through those bear market moments.

I had to smile. On March 20, 2020, with the stock market down 26 percent for the year, I got a text from her saying, "All that money in my 401(k) is gonna bounce back, right?"

I called her up, and we laughed together, but it got me thinking.

Today the Dow Jones Industrial Average is at about 26,000. In 25 years, Natalie will be 60 years old. If the stock market generates an annualized return of 6.5 percent for the next 25 years (a return significantly below its historical average), that would put the index at about 125,000 – maybe around the time Natalie starts contemplating retirement. I am not predicting that the stock market will appreciate that much, but I reminded her that what the stock market does over the next two years is irrelevant. Capturing as much of the stock market's return as she can over the next 25 years is essential to her life of wealth and happiness.

There is some good news for workers who participate in workplace retirement plans. As I mentioned earlier, many plans now offer "all-in-one" index funds, commonly referred to as target date funds. These investments automatically rebalance the stock/bond allocation over time, allowing you to focus more on your saving, not on your portfolio.

"I am smarter than Wall Street" is a narrative that can impact investors of all ages. Lisa, a 23-year-old college graduate, will soon begin contributing to her workplace retirement account. Thanks to a mom who has been a Coffeehouse Investor for the past 20 years and has shared the ground rules with her daughter, the confidence Lisa possesses in managing her own portfolio carries over to other dimensions of her life. Maybe it gives her added confidence for a bolder request on her first pay raise. Because Lisa has this investing thing down cold, the pay raise will be used to increase her saving in the company's workplace retirement plan.

It wouldn't surprise me if five years after Lisa starts contributing, the stock market drops 30 percent. Because Lisa has this investing thing down cold, while other investors are freaking out, Lisa will relish the opportunity to increase her contribution even more, knowing that a 30 percent drop in the market at her age serves her well in pursuing a life of wealth and happiness.

This change of narrative also impacts the life of Tina, a retired medical doctor. At 90, she lives her life as if the stock market doesn't exist. She is too busy connecting with her retirement community, sharing her good energy with its residents, and she figures out a way to share it, even amid the COVID-19 pandemic. The stock market's gyrations don't matter to her, because she has this investing thing down cold.

Twenty years ago, after reading my column for a year, Tina reached out to learn more. With a heavy heart, she revealed that her husband was bedridden, and his time left on Earth was short. Her anxiety about moving forward in life alone was matched by her determination to embrace the same wealth and happiness she had shared with him for 50 years.

Tina didn't need to play the game of Outfox the Box because she had already figured it out. Expecting to live a long time, she simply allocated enough of her portfolio in bonds to cover 10 years of withdrawals, reckoning that that allocation would outlast any bear market; and so far, it has. She manages her checkbook today with the same detail of 20 years ago. At 90, she has this investing thing down cold, giving her the freedom to do what she does best, nudging the global community forward by sharing her essential creativity within her community.

The change of narrative impacts the life of Denise and her husband, Patrick. They *both* have this investing thing down cold. Denise's story isn't unique, but it is powerful, because of the impact their shared decision had on their marriage and family finances. Her story reveals that she fell in love with a man who was absorbed in the stock market and took control managing their combined portfolios. His focus on the stock market carried over into other elements of their life. An imbalance of power unfolded, resulting from a sense that, when it came to finances, "he was smarter than her."

When I shared the simple game of Outfox the Box, Denise grasped its logic. She then shared the logic game with her husband, Patrick, and to his credit, he connected with it, as well. Now they both have this investing thing down cold. It allows them the freedom to address family-planning matters on an equal footing, like college education for their children, paying down the mortgage, increasing their life insurance, and maybe even saving more.

Denise and Patrick have created a spirit of trust on family financial issues that is elusive among couples. The open dialogue they cultivate by focusing on the checkbook and common sense is the legacy they will leave for their children in building a life of wealth and happiness.

The financial harmony created by Denise and Patrick is rare. In only 19 percent of households do partners share financial decisions equally; yet for those who do, the emotional benefits are overwhelming.

Of women who shared in long-term financial decisions,

- 95 percent responded, "If something happens to my spouse, I will already know all about our finances."
- 94 percent responded, "I'm more confident about our financial future."
- 93 percent responded, "We make fewer mistakes with both of us involved."
- 91 percent said, "I am less stressed about money."[5]

Not all relationships embrace a harmony like Denise and Patrick. In 2015 I connected with Peter and Carmen, and it was soon apparent that they owned a scattered approach to financial planning and portfolio management. With retirement five years out, they wanted to get on track.

Or so it seemed.

We talked about the benefits of creating a cohesive financial plan and Coffeehouse Investor-type portfolio, which would allow

---

[5]UBS. (2019). Own Your Worth. Why women should take control of their wealth to achieve financial well-being. *UBS Investor Watch – Global Insights: What's on Investors' Minds* 1.

them the liberty to focus all their energy on saving in the next five years until retirement. That is what Carmen wanted – a saving plan to get on track. While Carmen was quick to embrace the logic of Outfox the Box, Peter wasn't so sure. He seemed to think a higher level of attention was needed for a portfolio so close to retirement, especially during market downturns.

In the spring of 2016, after the stock market tumbled 18 percent, Peter was a wreck. He and Carmen were now four years from retirement and with the stock market going backward, they needed to make some quick adjustments to their portfolio, at least according to Peter.

When we discussed the inevitable market corrections, Carmen didn't have much to say, while Peter went on about the economy and things.

Then, with a shrug of her shoulders, Carmen quietly said, "This anxiety is consuming our lives."

Financial struggles and differences in the way partners look at managing portfolios is one of the biggest issues in a marriage. For couples who do embrace the ground rules, I have seen the meaningful impact it has on their lives.

You would think that more couples would be headed in that direction. Unfortunately, younger women are more likely than older women to defer family financial planning issues to their partner.

Following is the breakdown for women who defer financial planning issues to spouses, by age groups:

59 percent of women age 20–34

59 percent of women age 35–50

55 percent of women age 51+[6]

We have it in us to change the narrative for *both* women and men. You are smarter than Wall Street. Coffeehouse Investors have proven it. Now is your time to embrace it.

Whenever I think of changing the narrative, I think of my childhood farming community in Colton, Washington.

Like many little farming towns across the United States, sports are a big part of the social fabric. I have lots of good memories of those Friday night football games, and along the way, we won a few state championships. The last one was extra special – the *first* high school game played in that old concrete jungle known as Seattle's Kingdome.

While the boys were winning all those state championships, the girls at Colton High School were not winning much of anything. The narrative was that the girls just weren't that good at sports. As we got on with our lives, some of those buddies of mine, including my brother, returned to that town to farm, got married, and started families. Yep, you guessed it, the moms and dads started to have lots of little girls.

For those parents, changing the narrative started by opening the gym when the little girls were old enough to dribble a basketball, and letting them dribble a basketball.

---

[6]UBS. (2019). Own Your Worth. Why women should take control of their wealth to achieve financial well-being. *UBS Investor Watch – Global Insights: What's on Investors' Minds* 1.

Nothing too complicated about that. Open the gym and let them dribble. Those little girls laughed, had fun, and dribbled basketballs. As those girls grew up, they kept on dribbling basketballs, and eventually started playing little girl basketball games against neighboring towns – and winning some, too.

Those little girl basketball games became big girl basketball games, and they started winning at the high school level. In 2009, they won the state championship. The next year they won another state championship. And the same thing happened the next year and the year after that. The Colton High School girls' basketball team ended up winning nine state championships in 10 years. Oh, and when the girls weren't playing basketball they won six state championships in softball.

Talk about changing the narrative.

For the past 20 years, Coffeehouse Investors have been changing the narrative of investing. We can't let up now. Wouldn't it be great if someday every 22-year-old woman and man had this investing thing down cold in pursuit of a life of wealth and happiness?

It is possible. Let's take a closer look.

4

Ground Rule 2: Invest

John Kennedy once said,

> *The great enemy of truth is very often not the lie – deliberate,*
> *contrived and dishonest – but the myth – persistent, persuasive,*
> *and unrealistic.*

When it comes to investing in the stock market, the myth is that
great companies make great investments.

Nothing could be further from the truth.

That will never stop investors from trying to find those great companies. Just because it seems like everyone else is pursuing the myth doesn't mean you have to follow along. Let's explore this myth, the impact it could have on your portfolio, and, more importantly, the impact it could have on your life.

Beth and Mark wanted to talk business. They were set to embark on a new adventure in their careers, and it was time to get on track. Toward the end of our meeting, Beth quietly told me that the stock market caused her to feel anxious, stemming from her father's tortured experience of buying and selling stocks. She lived in a household where the mood at the dinner table was set by the gyrations of the stock market that day.

We spent a few minutes reflecting on those memories, and the journey many investors take to common stock ownership. We weighed the daunting task of buying and selling stocks over a lifetime of investing versus the benefits of buying all the stocks and holding them forever. Intellectually, I think she got it. Emotionally, I'm not so sure. I thought about telling her my own story, but didn't. Sometimes I wish I had.

The story behind *The Coffeehouse Investor* is one that unfolded with my own father while growing up on the wheat fields of the Palouse.

Like any young boy, I wanted to connect with my father. I guess I just wanted to sit on his knee and have him ask me, "Hey, how's it going? You are doing great things with your life, and tell me what you are working on today."

The problem with my father was, he had it backward. Early on, I figured out that the only way I was going to connect with him was for me to do the asking. "Hey Dad, how's it going? You are doing great things with your life, and tell me what you are working on today."

That is pretty much how things went in our relationship, until finally I quit trying to connect with him on his life and got on with my own.

I am not the only one who has struggled to connect with a father. Looking back, I am blessed beyond measure, because I had a mother who *still* turns to her 8 children and 20 grandchildren and asks them, "Hey, how's it going? You are doing great things with your life, and tell me what you are working on today."

My father was consumed with expanding the farm to be the biggest in Whitman County. That was important to him. He always wanted to be the best, and there is nothing wrong with that, but only when it is a healthy pursuit for you and the ones you love.

For him, it wasn't.

He worked closely with his brother to expand the farming operation. They were on their way to achieving that goal, until his brother decided he wanted to spend more time with his family and less time trying to be the biggest and the best.

That didn't set well with my father. He and my uncle decided to split up their farming operation and go it alone, which they did, after what seemed like 20 years of battling in court to draw up the new property lines.

Going it alone as a farmer only heightened my father's obsession with getting rich from the stock market. He was obsessed with trading stocks. Reflecting on it now, he was more than obsessed. Like Beth's dad, it tortured him. To get his children interested in the stock market he bought each child one share of stock in one company – companies like Chrysler, Dictaphone, Ronson, Pittson, and Boeing are a few that I remember.

He tried to figure out the stock market from different angles. He subscribed to the *Wall Street Journal* and *Forbes* magazine. He pored over stock-picking newsletters and trend-following services. When that didn't pan out he traveled to Portland, Oregon, and met up with a stockbroker who promoted himself as the no. 1 stock-picker in the Northwest. When that didn't work out, he fired him and hired another stockbroker in Spokane. That didn't last long either, so my father connected with a commodities broker and started trading commodities, and that was a disaster.

I was his confidant, every step of the way.

Later in life, when I was working as a stockbroker, my father assisted in establishing an endowment fund for the Catholic school attached to his church and, to no one's surprise, became chairman of the investment committee.

Along the way, he decided to invest a chunk of those endowment funds in a fast-growing Northwest company called Microsoft. As the stock appreciated over the years, that software company was just about all the endowment fund needed to support the work of the Lord, or so he thought.

After I stepped away from Wall Street and started working on my book, he frequently reminded me of the impressive growth of St. Gall's endowment fund.

The irony was that soon after *The Coffeehouse Investor* was published, Microsoft's stock started a 10-year slide; the price dropped by half, even though the company's earnings continued to soar.

My father couldn't figure that out. For him, it was a painful introduction to the efficiency of markets, where he learned that the emotions of investors, not the underlying earnings of a company, can drive the price of a stock for a very long time.

During that stretch I came to realize that my father wasn't intent on maximizing returns in the stock market. Buying and selling stocks was a hobby to him, and his hobby in his personal life carried over to management of St. Gall's endowment fund.

For his household finances, the farm income and Social Security benefits meant that he and my mother would always be able to pay their bills while living out there on the banks of the Snake River. He didn't need to maximize returns in the stock market.

For my brothers and sisters, who can't count on a farm income to supplement their monthly Social Security checks, investing shouldn't be a hobby. It is serious stuff.

Over the past 20 years, enough Coffeehouse Investors have revealed to me that Beth's father and my father were not the only fathers consumed with their hobby of trading stocks.

I am not knocking my father's fascination with the stock market. I think you would agree that we have a culture that is captivated with the stock market, and it's only getting worse, with free trading and online access. That doesn't mean we must follow along.

I admit that the stock market is a fascinating component and an integral part of economies around the world. We are blessed to live in a society that allows good ideas to percolate in our imaginations, and an economic system that allows us to create companies and bring those ideas to the stock markets of capitalism.

Even though capitalism creates its own problems, it is still a pretty good system for improving the lives of our global community, and we explore ways to make it even better in Chapter 8.

The stock market allows private companies to offer shares of stock for sale to the public. This allows the company access to money that can be used for a variety of purposes, including the expansion and future growth of the business.

As Beth and I discussed, and what our fathers discovered, is the disconnect between the profitability of a company and the price of its publicly traded stock. Understanding this difference guides us in how we structure our portfolios and gives us the freedom to ignore the gyrations of individual common stocks while participating in its collective long-term growth.

First, let's talk about a "company." I love the idea of a company, even if it means a company of one, because someone has taken an idea and introduced it to the world. It reflects our relentless human spirit and essential creativity to nudge the global community forward. For instance, my mother's daydream was to raise children, and she was good at it. When her last child went off to college, she started a company of one, a child daycare, and called it "Grandma Annie's." Lots of parents in that little farming town wanted to have their children raised at Grandma Annie's and she turned it into a thriving little business. A few years back, when I was out to dinner with her, sitting at the table next to us was a family of four. When the father saw us, he came over to our table, gave my mother a hug, and told her that she'd had a big impact on his life. I am guessing that every day when he was dropped off at her daycare, she gave him a hug and asked, "Hey, how's it going? You are doing great things with your life, and tell me what you are working on today."

Sometimes a company moves beyond a company of one and becomes a multinational company with thousands of employees. I love watching this Energy of the Universe unfold, especially with companies in the Northwest.

I wake up in the morning and lace up my shoes purchased at Nordstrom. I buy groceries at Costco. I grab coffee at Starbucks. I work on computers and software created by Microsoft. At night, a package is delivered to my door by Amazon. If I go on a trip, I'll fly Alaska Air on a jet built by Boeing.

Every working day for the past 20 years, I have had a five-minute morning ritual of scanning the headlines of the *Wall Street Journal* and the *New York Times,* not to keep up with the stock market, but because I want to keep up with companies. I want to keep up with the dynamics of change. I want to keep up with life.

For example, I'm interested in companies that are focused on producing, processing, and delivering food – a basic human need. Maybe it is the farmer in me, but I love watching companies try to keep up with the demands of consumers: autonomous tractors; safer chemicals; enhanced food processing plants; redesigned supermarkets; pre-prepped food; food delivery companies; fast food restaurants offering fresh salads; sit-down restuarants offering takeout. It is the never-ending change that nudges the global community forward.

Awhile back a Coffeehouse Investor friend of mine, who worked his entire life in the food distribution business, predicted that in 10 years there will be only two companies in the food business, and I'll let you guess which they are. His prediction might just come to pass, but you'd better believe there are a lot of companies scrambling to make sure that doesn't happen.

Enough about companies. Let's talk about stocks. Let's talk about Starbucks. Everyone in Seattle seems to own at least a few shares of Starbucks. As an owner of Starbucks stock, you can make money in two ways: receiving a dividend, and by selling the stock at a profit to someone else who wants to own Starbucks.

Here's where things get a little confusing for some investors. While Starbucks the company controls the dividend, Starbucks the company has no control over the price of its stock.

The price of its stock is set by the buyers and sellers in the stock market, people like you and me who think the price of Starbucks is going to go up or go down. For this discussion, let's say that you, as a buyer of their stock, expect Starbucks to continue its growth of opening coffeehouses around the world, and you want to be part of that growth.

The good news is that Starbucks is likely to continue its world-wide growth. The bad news for you is that you aren't the only person who's thought of buying shares of Starbucks to participate in this growth. Thousands of investors with the same idea have already bid up the price of Starbucks stock so that most of the expected future growth of the Starbucks company is already factored into the current stock price.

When you decide to buy the stock of Starbucks, you aren't really making a bet that Starbucks the company will continue to grow. You are making a bet that you are smarter than the collective wisdom of thousands of other investors who have already weighed in by purchasing or selling the stock of Starbucks.

That is the painful lesson my father learned with the stock of Microsoft during the period 2000 to 2009. To Microsoft's credit, it is one of the few technology companies that has been able to skillfully navigate this thing called change, and the price of the stock now reflects this.[1]

A couple of years after I started writing my Coffeehouse column in the *King County Journal*, a reader in her late 70s reached out to me, wanting to learn more. Mary and her deceased husband had built up a sizable investment portfolio of stocks and bonds to complement their commercial real estate holdings. They were intent on leaving a part of their legacy to their 34 grandchildren. Mary's warmth of spirit reminded me of my own mother's warm embrace of life. Mary confided in me that one of her joys was buying and selling stocks and following the stock market.

Knowing that her grandchildren would be partial recipients of her investment portfolio, she wanted to learn more about index funds to share the investing philosophy with them.

Introducing the logic of owning the entire stock market through index funds is an interesting exercise, because the wisdom of owning all the companies instead of picking individual companies can be hard to grasp for investors who are set in their ways.

For some, an hour's explanation isn't enough. For Mary, it took about three minutes. On a piece of paper I sketched five stocks, each trading at $1/share. It looked like this:

---

[1]For a more complete review of the dynamics of change in industry, please see Richard Foster and Sarah Kaplan's *Creative Destruction* in the Further Reading.

Not knowing in advance how any of them will perform over the next 20 years, let's assume that two companies will appreciate in price to $100 a share, two companies will trade at $2 share, and one company will remain at $1.

It looked like this:

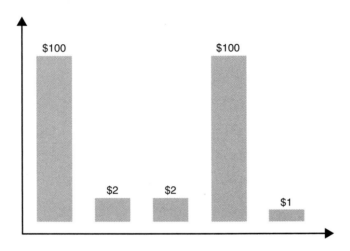

I asked Mary, if she had $5,000 to invest today, how would she allocate her dollars?

She smiled, and said, "I'd own them all."

A primary benefit of index funds is their low cost structure. Less understood is the dynamics of the underlying stocks themselves. Over time, a select few stocks will outperform and drive the markets higher. Hendrik Bessembinder, professor at Arizona State University, published a paper titled, "Do Stocks Outperform T-Bills?" His research found that:

- All of the dollar wealth creation in the public US stock market since 1926 can be attributed to slightly more than

4 percent of stocks, and over half the value creation can be attributed to .36 percent of the stocks.

- This means that 96 percent of stocks collectively matched T-bills, while 4 percent did better and created wealth to the overall market.[2]

Is that time period too long for you? Research conducted by Dimensional Fund Advisors looked at the best performing stocks on global stock market returns over the period from January 1994 to December 2019. For this analysis, they excluded the top 10 percent of names across all regions with the highest cumulative returns over the period. Excluding the top 10 percent of performing stocks reduced the cumulative return from 640 percent to 208 percent.[3]

	All Stocks	**Excluding Top 10%**	**Top 10%**
Cumulative Return	640%	208%	2288%
Growth of $1	$7.40	$3.08	$23.88

Even though Mary continued to enjoy buying individual stocks, I think she got more joy from sharing the simple logic of index funds with her 34 grandchildren, and explaining that the optimal way of investing in the stock market is to own all the companies for the rest of their lives.

Mary has since passed away. While the financial legacy she left her 34 grandchildren was meaningful, the emotional freedom she

[2]Bessembinder, Hendrik. (2018). Do stocks outperform Treasury bills? *Journal of Financial Economics* 129 (3): 440–457.
[3]Dimensional Fund Advisors. (2020). Exhibit 1: Global stock market performance excluding top performers, 1994–2019.

bestowed on them by allowing them to focus on their essential creativity instead of the stock market may have been her greatest gift of all.

The Energy of the Universe invites all of us to share the same wisdom of investing with people who yearn for a life of wealth and happiness. The person you share it with might not have a grandmother with the good sense of Mary.

They might have an uncle named Fred.

In February 2019 I was on vacation, and went down early one morning to get a cup of coffee at a local coffeehouse. I struck up a conversation with Fred, a newly retired high school math teacher. It didn't take long for the conversation to turn to picking stocks. He was quick to share with me that his passion in life, after teaching math classes, was analyzing companies in his stock portfolio. He was not shy telling me that his early retirement was largely a result of his shrewd stock-picking skills of Amazon, Apple, and Microsoft.

He proceeded to tell me that one of his greatest accomplishments as a high school math teacher was establishing a stock picking class within the high school curriculum. He was convinced that analyzing and selecting companies was an essential life skill that needed to be taught to every high school student, and was working with the local community college to establish a similar curriculum.

I decided to humor myself, and briefly brought up the idea of "owning all the companies," but he wouldn't have it, and we both went on to enjoy our vacations.

Sadly, there are too many Freds who have a stock-picking agenda directed at too many young investors. Stock-picking classes abound at high schools and colleges. A quick online search included the following description:

> *The purpose of the project is to teach high school students the value to investing and using the stock market. This project also teaches important lessons about the economy, mathematics, and financial responsibility.*
>
> *The basis of this project is to learn about the stock market while investing a specified amount of fake money in certain stocks. Students then study the results and buy and sell as they see fit.*
>
> *As a teacher, your job is to guide the students and provide them with the supplies necessary to successfully monitor stock market trends. Teachers must also teach students how to calculate profit and loss on stocks.*

If someone wants to teach a personal finance class as part of a life-skills class, the best place to start is by teaching them to add and subtract – you know, the complicated math of managing a checkbook. For the stock market portion of the class, have them play a quick game of Outfox the Box covered in Chapter 3.

Then, have each student figure out a starting salary for their career job and calculate on an Excel spreadsheet what it looks like saving 15 percent of their paycheck compounded at 5 percent over 40 years.

The obsession with picking stocks doesn't stop at the high school level. Later that year, I connected with the director of a major university's financial planning program, to inquire about possible candidates for our wealth management firm. He acknowledged the joy he receives in analyzing companies for portfolios, and in teaching students the same critical analysis. I can only guess that some of his students, in a financial planning career, will spend more time following stocks than on the clients' financial planning issues that matter most of all.

Our culture's fascination with picking stocks runs deep. Stock-trading courses flourish, in hotel conference rooms and online trading seminars. Televised stock-picking programs, with moderators barking predictions to buy and sell the stocks of the day, are entertaining for some but have nothing to do with building a portfolio that works for a lifetime.

Paul Newman as Eddie in *The Color of Money* said, "Money won is twice as sweet as money earned."

There will always be those investors who enjoy trading stocks, egged on by financial institutions that offer commission-free trades and sleek apps. On a positive note, many of these same financial institutions have created investor-friendly investments like target-date funds for investors who are seeking intelligent building blocks for portfolios.

Most target-date funds consist of broad-based market index funds, with an allocation between stocks and bonds targeted to a specific "retirement" date. As the investor gets closer to retirement, the fund automatically rebalances from stocks to bonds to create a more conservative portfolio.

A target-date mutual fund benefits you in at least three ways.

1. *Maximize portfolio returns*. As John Bogle was fond of saying, you "get your fair share" of stock market returns.

2. *Allows you to focus on your financial plan*. Knowing you are getting your fair share of market returns, you can now focus on your financial plan, including clarity on whether your savings of today will cover your expenses in retirement.

Does your financial plan have a tax management strategy for accumulating dollars and withdrawing dollars? Have you reviewed your insurance planning, eldercare planning, and estate planning? Keep in mind that with a target-date fund you still need to be aware of its allocation between stocks and bonds so the fund reflects the short-term risk you can and need to take to reach your financial goals.

3. *Allow you to get on with your life*. Coffeehouse Investors turn their attention away from the stock market and toward their life of wealth and happiness.

- Save
- Invest
- Plan

Jane Goodall said,

> *"What you do makes a difference. And you have to decide what kind of difference you want to make."*

Over the past 20 years, like Mary, Coffeehouse Investors have made a difference by taking it upon themselves to share a simple investing wisdom with others.

You can make a difference by first embracing these principles and then sharing these principles with the same missionary-like zeal as John Bogle and Burton Malkiel. You don't have to be a Coffeehouse Investor to share them. Get creative and think of a name to call it as if it is your own message, because it is. Some people call themselves Bogleheads. Some are attached to a FIRE movement. As Larry Swedroe, prolific writer and director of Buckingham Asset Management, is fond of saying, "We *can* change the world, one investor at a time."

5

Wall Street Unwound

I love the game of golf, and the older I get the worse I play; but I know one thing for sure – it isn't the clubs.

I love the game because I love trying to figure it out, even though, deep down, I know I never will. That's what keeps me coming back for another 18 holes and another hour on the driving range.

There is no shortage of golfers who will give me tips on my golf swing; but the one tip that sticks with me was offered up by my hero, a golfer named Speedy.

Speedy is my hero not because he is a great golfer, although he is. Speedy is my hero because he is a great human being. He takes the time to care about people in his life, he cares about his community, and he cares about our country.

When we were playing golf a while back, halfway into the round Speedy sensed I was struggling (he's good at tuning in to the obvious). He paused, and then, in that southwestern drawl of his, told me to spend less time staring at what's in front of me (the ball), and more time visualizing the outcome.

Later on, he mailed me a book, *The Natural Golf Swing*, written by one of the greatest ball strikers you've never heard of, George Knutson.[1]

George Knutson played golf as if the golf ball wasn't there. He told a story about shooting a score of 67 with his eyes closed on full swings. In his book he goes on to say,

> *Having a clear image of the target in your mind gets you going. It gives you purpose, direction, and intent. How are you going to establish a route or a path to get somewhere if you haven't decided upon your destination? The more clearly you can fix your destination in your mind, the more easily will you reach your objective.*

If I didn't know any better, I would think George was commenting on the Coffeehouse ground rules.

Sometimes I wonder if George looked at the golfing industry in the same way I look at Wall Street. The golfing industry doesn't have a problem with you focusing on the thing in front of you, that little white ball. The more you focus on the little white ball instead of your purpose, direction, and intent, the more you might just consider the new set of golf clubs that will hit that

---

[1]Knutson, George & Lorne Rubenstein, (1988) The Natural Golf Swing, Toronto, CA, McClelland & Stewart Ltd.

little white ball a little farther and a lot straighter than the clubs you own today.

Wall Street operates the same way. I saw it 30 years ago, and I see it today.

In building a portfolio, Wall Street wants you to focus on what is in front of you – not your destination. For example, recently I reviewed a newsletter from a major Wall Street firm, and these were the items they wanted you to focus on:

- COVID-19 and its impact on the economy
- Government spending and inflation
- China's influence on Asia's recovery
- The shape of the US recovery

Even though we have redefined the ground rules of investing by tuning out Wall Street's agenda in favor of low-cost index funds, Wall Street wants to remain relevant in our lives.

From here on out, make Wall Street irrelevant. If George Knutson could shoot a 67 with his eyes closed, you can live your life as if Wall Street doesn't exist. Your pursuit of wealth and happiness is all about you and the ground rules. It's not about Wall Street.

Wall Street isn't the evil empire. The institution plays an essential role in the flow of capital, and allows us to invest in the collective creativity of human beings. That doesn't change a thing. Your wealth and happiness is all about you and the ground rules. It's not about Wall Street.

Sometimes it takes a little perseverance on your part to focus on you, because Wall Street can be a persuasive bunch. I learned that the hard way, and it started with a little bear named Teddy Ruxpin.

In 1986 this furry little creature became the toy world's no. 1 seller. It was produced by a company called Worlds of Wonder, whose stock symbol was WOW, and it was one of the stock market's fastest-growing companies at the time.[2]

I met Teddy Ruxpin not in a toy store, but in the office of Smith Barney in Seattle. I was working in a room called "the bullpen," cold-calling for more municipal bond clients, when my manager called me into his corner office. He told me that Smith Barney's over-the-counter trading desk had obtained several thousand shares of WOW stock, and we needed to sell it to our retail clients.

I don't remember how many shares I was allotted, but my manager made it clear to me that I wasn't going home until I sold those shares to my clients.

I walked back to the bullpen and started calling my municipal bond clients, many of whom had never bought a share of stock in their lives. I said, "Hey, let me tell you about a little teddy bear named Teddy Ruxpin." It was a tough sell and a long afternoon.

Those were the heydays of Wall Street, when commissions on small-company, over-the-counter securities were built into the price of the stocks. Stockbrokers could make big commissions trading those types of stocks for their clients.

I did not know what was going on behind the scenes, but looking back, I think some of the founders of WOW wanted to unload their stock and my clients were the unsuspecting victims, because, a couple of years later, WOW declared bankruptcy.

---

[2]Cuff, Daniel F. (1988). Worlds of Wonder loses its chairman. *New York Times* (April 4), p. 58.

Somehow, Teddy Ruxpin survived, and is still sold through retail toy channels.

Most of the stock-trading activity in those days was in blue-chip companies listed on traditional stock exchanges. Every morning before the stock market opened, Smith Barney's stock analysts updated their outlook on the companies they were covering. There was a lot of pressure on these stock analysts to secure a spot on the prestigious All-American Research Institutional Investor first-team selection. At times this pursuit was a little suspect, because the stockbrokers were never quite sure if the analysts' "buy" recommendations came from the stock's fundamental outlook, or from the cozy investment banking relationship the company had with Smith Barney.

Back then, there was another route to stock ownership. You could place your money with a professional stock picker – a mutual fund manager – and that was where being the best really paid off.

In the stock-picking arena of actively managed mutual funds, Fidelity's Peter Lynch was one of the best. From 1977 to 1990, his Magellan Fund generated an annualized return of 29.2 percent, more than doubling the returns of the Standard & Poor's 500 Index.

Competing with Peter Lynch were John Neff, who managed the Windsor fund at Vanguard, John Templeton at Templeton Funds, and other well-known stock pickers.

With so many mutual funds to choose from, who was the best stock picker for your portfolio? You could always pick up a copy of your favorite financial magazine while waiting in the checkout line of your grocery store. The December issues were always a favorite, advertising the top funds for the following year.

There had to be a better way.

In 1984, a young stock analyst named Joe Mansueto, tuning in to his essential creativity, came up with the idea of aggregating mutual fund data for investors to review in pursuit of building a better portfolio. He called his company Morningstar, and created a style box to categorize mutual funds, that looked like this:

Large Growth	**Large Blend**	**Large Value**
Mid-cap Growth	**Mid-cap Blend**	**Mid-cap Value**
Small Growth	**Small Blend**	**Small Value**

Morningstar also established a five-star fund ranking system that soon became everyone's new way of pursuing the top funds. The fund managers loved the stars, because a five-star ranking meant more fees from the dollars that poured in from investors chasing the five-star performance.

As a subscriber to Morningstar, the thing I liked best about its data was that the floppy discs I received in the mail could be downloaded onto an Excel spreadsheet. This gave me an opportunity to analyze historical fund performance, and my number-crunching confirmed what mutual fund companies were required by law to tell us: past performance is virtually meaningless as a method for choosing a top mutual fund.

Long before Burton Malkiel wrote his book *A Random Walk Down Wall Street*, long before John Bogle started Vanguard, and long before Joe Mansueto started Morningstar, there were others who questioned the usefulness of using past performance as a selection tool for securities in a portfolio.

Let's go all the way back to 1900, when a French mathematician, Louis Bachelier, suggested in his PhD thesis, "The Theory of Speculation," that stock price movement was random.

Let's go back to 1933, when Alfred Cowles III, heir to the *Chicago Tribune* fortune, in discussing stock market forecasters, stated, "Statistical tests of the best individual records fail to demonstrate that they exhibited skill, and indicate that they more probably were the result of chance."[3]

Let's go back to 1960, when young economist Edward Renshaw and an MBA student, Paul Feldstein, co-authored a paper titled "The Case for an Unmanaged Investment Company," and submitted it to the *Financial Analysts Journal*.

Introducing the thesis, they wrote . . .

> *The problem of choice and supervision originally created a need for investment companies has so mushroomed these institutions that today a case can be made for creating a new investment institution, what we have chosen to call an "unmanaged investment company" – in other words a company dedicated to the task of following a representative average.*

Later in the paper they added these comments:

> *While a great deal of information on investment companies has been collected in recent years and analyzed in terms of performance no one has seriously questioned two of the basic axioms of investment company policy: notably, that professional advice and continued supervision are worth their price.*[4]

---

[3]Cowles, Alfred III. (1933). Rates luck above Wall St. experts. As quoted in the *New York Times* (January 1), p. 7.
[4]*Financial Analysts Journal* (January/February 1960).

A few months after their paper was published, in the same journal, a securities analyst named John Armstrong wrote a rebuttal to Renshaw and Feldstein's work. His paper, titled "The Case for Mutual Fund Management," spelled out a strong argument for professional stock pickers as the preferred method of investing in the stock market.

To conclude, Armstrong wrote,

> *It is clear that even the most assiduous analysis of yesterday's figures cannot foretell what tomorrow may bring – whether the problem is selecting a mutual fund or an individual investment, or forecasting the action of the stock market, or indeed of predicting any event dependent on the human element. However, the Financial Analyst – and the mutual fund shareholder – can gain confidence from the fact that mutual funds in general have met the test of time and performed in keeping with their stated policies and goal.*[5]

John Armstrong was actually the pen name used by Vanguard founder John Bogle, who, at the time, was a rising star with the Wellington Management Company, a mutual fund firm.

Over the next decade, the idea of an unmanaged investment company continued to percolate on Wall Street and in Academia, led by a band of free-market economists at the University of Chicago.

Utilizing added computing power that was now available, researchers were able to quantify what had been largely theory: that professional stock pickers have a hard time consistently outperforming benchmark indices.

---

[5] *Financial Analysts Journal* (May/June 1960).

This observation became known as the Efficient Market Hypothesis, a concept we discussed in Chapter 4. Stock prices reset throughout the day by the countless transactions of investors who weigh in on a company's future. The result? Much of the company's future is already (and efficiently) priced into a stock's price.

Despite the growing focus on efficient markets, the 1960s were tagged the "Go-Go" years by market pundits, and professional stock pickers continued to dominate Wall Street. Behind the scenes, work was unfolding to implement the idea of efficient markets with an unmanaged investment company by introducing an "index fund" type of investment to institutional investors.

In 1969, William Fouse, a manager at Mellon National Bank & Trust, tried to convince the bank's trust department to create an index trust for the bank's institutional clients. Mellon Bank chose not to pursue it, which resulted in Mr. Fouse joining Wells Fargo Bank. He and his new colleagues, including Mac McQuown, who led the technical work, established the first commercially available index investment for the pension plan of the Samsonite Luggage company.

While the index fund concept was unfolding with institutional accounts, retail investors like you and me were left out.

In 1973, Burton Malkiel wrote his *A Random Walk Down Wall Street*, bringing the idea of efficient markets to individual investors. His writing served as a catalyst for John Bogle at Vanguard to create the first index fund for retail investors in 1976.

Vanguard's index fund was roundly criticized throughout Wall Street, but started to capture the attention of investors in the years that followed.

In 1981, while Vanguard was growing its S&P 500 index fund, two graduates of the University of Chicago, Rex Sinquefield and David Booth, started a company called Dimensional Fund Advisors (DFA).[6] Armed with research showing the historical benefits of diversifying a common stock portfolio beyond large company stocks, they built an index fund focused on small-company stocks.

Rolf Banz, also from the University of Chicago, found that small-company stocks generated higher returns than large-company stocks, and suggested that this anomaly occurred because small-company stocks were riskier, and thus investors demanded a higher return for owning these companies.

Here is where the world of Wall Street and Academia gets interesting.

Efficient market theorists suggest that you can't consistently beat the market, but if you own riskier stocks, you can beat the market. In other words, you can't beat the market, but you can beat the market.

Have I got that straight?

Somewhere, somehow, Wall Street has come unwound. Over the years the pursuit of the top stock picker has morphed into the pursuit of the top index fund. Like I said earlier, even though we have redefined the ground rules of investing by using low-cost index funds as building blocks for our portfolios, that hasn't changed Wall Street's obsession with trying to stay relevant in our lives.

---

[6]DFA website, www.us.dimensional.com.

On May 30, 1992, Standard & Poor's Corporation created two new indexes to track value stocks and growth stocks, and by November 2, 1992, Vanguard had established the corresponding Value Index Fund and Growth Index fund.

1992 was also the year that two professors at the University of Chicago, Eugene Fama and Ken French (now at Dartmouth), produced a paper titled "The Cross-Section of Expected Stock Returns."

Their work found that the returns of your portfolio will be impacted by three factors, known as the three-factor model:

1. The total amount of common stocks in your portfolio.
2. The amount of small-cap stocks in your portfolio.
3. The amount of value stocks in your portfolio.

Following up on this research, in 1992 DFA created a value fund and small value fund for investors intent on capturing this expected higher return (premium).

The plot thickens. Not everyone on Wall Street and in Academia agreed with the research of Fama and French. Some suggested instead that the expected premium of small and value stocks wasn't a risk factor, it was a behavioral factor. Small and value stocks were underpriced and ignored compared to the faster-growing large-company stocks endorsed by the stock-picking analysts on Wall Street.

Is it a risk story or is it a behavior story, does it even matter, and should you include these factors in your portfolio?

I'll let you decide.

When I moved to Seattle, Washington, in 1983, I lived in a fun little neighborhood called Queen Anne, just north of downtown Seattle. A couple of blocks from my apartment was a grimy little grocery store that carried the essentials – you know, the six-pack of beer or pint of ice cream you needed late on a Saturday night. Dust covered the soup cans, and the guy behind the counter didn't pay much attention to me because he was glued to his black-and-white TV.

Ten years after I moved to Queen Anne, developers moved in, leveled a city block a couple of blocks from Grimy's, and built a hip new grocery store we'll call Mike's. It was one of the coolest grocery stores in Seattle, kind of a precursor to Whole Foods.

Neither Grimy's nor Mike's was publicly traded, but let's say for a moment that they were. When deciding which stock to purchase, especially after hearing that Mike's was super-successful and expected to expand all over Seattle, which grocery store would *you* want to own?

Well, a dollar earned is a dollar earned, whether it is earned at Grimy's or Mike's. But, being the emotional humans that we are, we tend to prefer cool grocery stores that are expected to expand all over the place, especially compared to the little grocery store down the street. On top of that, there are plenty of Wall Street analysts enamored with Mike's who are telling us to buy the fast-growing company.

Those who say the expected premium of value and small stocks is a behavioral factor will tell you that investors have simply bid up the stock price of Mike's to a level that exceeds its future growth potential.

Those who say the expected premium is a risk factor will say that Grimy's is riskier than Mike's and as such, investors demand a higher return.

By now you are probably saying, "Hey, wait a minute! If I own an index fund, don't I own both Grimy's and Mike's?"

Well, you kind of do, but you kind of don't in a traditional market-capitalization-weighted index. If Mike's market capitalization is $200 and Grimy's is $2, you would own 100 times more Mike's than Grimy's in your portfolio. So, you might as well just own Mike's.

Some will say that owning the entire stock market, based on market capitalization, is the simplest and smartest way to own common stocks. Others will say you should own a little more of Grimy's than what you get in a total stock market index, not only because of the expected added return of Grimy's, but because there can be extended periods of time that Grimy's will outperform Mike's.

Not all of the time, but some of the time.

In my first book, *The Coffeehouse Investor*, I addressed both approaches by saying that a total stock market index fund is a smart way to invest in the stock market. If you want to take that diversification strategy one small step further, invest in value index funds and small-cap index funds as well. I wrote,

> *Keep in mind that if you choose to add value, small value, and REIT index funds to your portfolio, you are doing nothing more than fine-tuning an already good thing. It simply takes*

this thing we are talking about – diversification – one (small) step further.[7]

For the first ten years after I started writing my weekly Coffeehouse Investor column, the small and value factors performed as advertised, providing a premium return compared to the overall stock market, and the factor fans (they are a vocal bunch) proclaimed, "Hey, these factors are great!"

Since then, the small and value factors have underperformed the total stock market index, and the anti-factor crowd (they are a vocal bunch) proclaim, "Hey, these factors aren't so great!"

Whether or not you are a factor fan, factors are here to stay. Factors have mushroomed into so many more factors like momentum and profitability that I can't keep track of them.

Besides, I'd rather work on my golf game.

Not long after value and small value index funds appeared on the scene, a new type of investment emerged, labeled the exchange-traded fund (ETF), forever transforming the mutual fund industry. The first ETF, created in 1993, was called a Spider, symbol SPY, that tracked the S&P 500 index.

The traditional way of buying and selling mutual funds was a transaction that took place at the end of the trading day.

SPY allowed investors to purchase the S&P 500 index at the prevailing price throughout the day. Over the next 10 years,

---

[7]Schultheis, Bill (2009). The New Coffeehouse Investor, New York, The Penguin Group.

international ETFs, small-cap ETFs, value ETFs, and factor-based ETFs started trading on stock exchanges. All types of ETFs were to follow, including bond ETFs, sustainable ETFs, and commodity ETFs, just to name a few.

Leave it to Wall Street to take the simple concept of index funds and turn it inside out. Now, instead of picking stocks to beat the market, investors are picking ETFs to beat the market.

Dimensional Fund Advisors and Vanguard have been pioneers in providing "factor" strategies to the universe of index funds. Almost every major Wall Street institution now offers some type of index fund in an ETF format covering the growing array of factors. Wall Street is a persuasive bunch, suggesting that their factors can hit that little white ball a little farther and a little straighter.

Or something like that.

In looking at which approach is better for you, a total stock market index fund or a portfolio that incorporates additional factors, I want to share a little secret with you. I swim like I play golf. Neither one is pretty.

My family's farm out on the Palouse overlooks the majestic Snake River. Back when I was a kid, before the Army Corps of Engineers built the Lower Granite Dam, it was a swift-running river, not conducive to learning how to swim. That didn't stop my brothers and sisters and me from wanting to learn. One year a big windstorm blew down one of our grain silos. My brother and I disassembled the silo, ring by ring, and then sunk one of the metal rings into the ground. We filled it with water and had ourselves a swimming pool.

I'm still not much of a swimmer.

In the spring of 2016, I traveled to Florida to see a good friend of mine, Steve, who took me deep sea fishing. We were trolling for fish in the open ocean, and before we knew it, four fish were fighting on the lines. Chaos broke loose, and as we were trying to reel them in, my palms were sweaty and I was thinking to myself, "I can barely swim." I had a great time, and it was a great memory for a kid who tried to learn how to swim in a torn-down grain silo 3,000 miles away.

Before I returned to Seattle, I stopped by to see another friend in south Florida, a gentleman named Taylor Larimore. Taylor is a giant of a man who fought in the Battle of the Bulge, and, later in life, along with Mel Lindauer, established an online forum called "Bogleheads" in honor of Jack Bogle. Taylor still contributes to the Bogleheads forum and the example he sets with his courteous exchange of ideas mirrors the exchange of other like-minded investors on the forum who have helped thousands embrace simple ground rules for life.

On this Saturday, Taylor invited me on his sailboat to race in Biscayne Bay. I loved every minute of it, but Taylor could sense the obvious, that I barely know how to swim. Watching him command that sailing vessel across beautiful Biscayne Bay while keeping one eye on me is a memory I will hold onto for life.

On the Boglehead forum, Taylor Larimore is an enthusiastic advocate of owning the entire stock market as part of a three-fund portfolio highlighted in his wonderful book, *The Boglehead's Guide to the Three-Fund Portfolio*. Factor investing doesn't have a place in his portfolio. He recognizes the wisdom of simplicity and shares it with others.

I, however, prefer to complement a total stock market portfolio by also including a value index fund and small-company index fund. I recognize that there will be periods when different dimensions of the market will underperform others and prefer to hedge my emotions short term, if not my returns long term. I am not sure I could stay the course with a total stock market fund if there is another ten-year period like 1999–2008 when that fund languished, compared to all the rest.

We went sailing that memorable morning and we never discussed the nuances of our respective approaches, *because it didn't matter*. We had better things to talk about, like our families, our careers, our lives, and our journey of redefining this thing called investing.

If you embrace the major theme of low-cost, low-turnover funds with market efficiencies and tax efficiencies, *it doesn't matter* how you build your portfolio; whether you use DFA, Vanguard, Charles Schwab, J.P. Morgan, Goldman Sachs, Fidelity, Avantis, or Capital Group funds.

What does matter is that you stay the course with what you embrace, especially when the portfolio you embrace doesn't seem to be the strategy that is working at the moment.

A primary benefit of "staying the course," as Jack Bogle would say, is that you maximize returns in each basket, or asset class, within your portfolio.

A far greater benefit is that it allows you the emotional freedom to turn away from Wall Street things and focus on your financial plan.

That's what we'll talk about next.

After I get back from the driving range.

6

Ground Rule 3: *Your* Plan

Creating a financial plan to see you through 25 years of unemployment, called retirement, is like descending through a heavy cloud cover to land your airplane. The secret is to dial in your power settings and make small adjustments along the way.

That is what my flight instructors shared with me. That is what I'm sharing with you.

Nicole, my first instructor, spent the first three sessions on power settings. "Bill, you've got to dial in your power settings and make small adjustments along the way."

A year later, Natalie said the same thing. "First, let's figure out your power settings, and then make small corrections – you have to remain stable down the glide slope."

Mark told me: "Bill, first you need to set your power settings. It makes it easier to make small adjustments to get back on track."

David was a little firmer. "It makes flying the airplane so much easier if you just get your power settings dialed in first, allowing you to make small adjustments and remain stable."

Descending through the thick marine cloud cover over Elliott Bay, then breaking out of the clouds at 800 feet to see the runway at Boeing Field in Seattle, is one of the greatest feelings in the world. At least for me.

I have connected with enough Coffeehouse Investors to see the same satisfaction when they are on track with their financial plan.

Dial in those power settings:

- Your savings today.
- Your expected spending in retirement.
- The expected increase of your spending, otherwise known as your personal inflation rate.
- The expected growth rate of your portfolio.

. . . and make small adjustments along the way.

Let's look at these power settings, the impact they have on your financial plan, and the significance of making small adjustments along the way.

Just as I relied on several different flight instructors to finally obtain my instrument flight rating, you will probably explore several different retirement calculators before settling on one that works for you. I have seen one-page financial plans that work and 40-page financial plans that don't work because they are so complicated you can't even locate the power settings.

Regardless of which retirement calculator you select, you need to understand the impact of your power settings, the location of your power settings in your calculator, and then get those power settings dialed in.

Your primary goal in creating a financial plan is to get on track and stay on track. Will the amount you are saving today, combined with your Social Security and other income, cover your expenses in retirement? Let's look at how each power setting impacts your financial plan.

Dialing in your power settings means it is time to start tracking your saving and spending, as we discussed in Chapter 2. It is pretty simple, really. Your monthly spending in retirement drives how much you need to save today. The amount you are spending today is a *good first guess* of how much you are likely to be spending in retirement, adjusted for any major costs, like mortgages and healthcare expenses.

Maybe, as a new college graduate, you are just starting to save, and have no idea how much your monthly burn rate will be in retirement. That's okay. Start saving 10 percent, 20 percent, or whatever you can, and take a guess at your monthly spending in retirement. Enter your saving and expected spending into your planning calculator, and then make small adjustments along the way.

Next year, do the same thing. Enter your saving and expected retirement spending into your planning calculator, and then make small adjustments along the way to get on track and stay on track.

The following year, do it again. Enter your saving and expected retirement spending into your planning calculator, and then make small adjustments along the way.

Do you see a pattern here?

It might be next year, it might be 10 years from now, it might be 10 years from retirement, it might be at retirement. If you review your flight plan year after year and adjust your power settings along the way, your expectations for retirement will converge on the reality that unfolds when you do retire.

This idea of getting on track and then staying on track by making small adjustments along the way is no different than maintaining a stable glide path on your descent in cloudy weather.

If you never get on track, or if you get on track and then start drifting, and you don't make small adjustments to get back on track, and you are in a thick layer of clouds, lots of bad things can happen.

At least that's what they told me in flight school.

Now let's explore the power setting that fuels your financial plan – the expected growth rate of your portfolio. Somewhere in your retirement calculator, you will be prompted to either (1) default to the software's preset rate of return, (2) rely on the software's Monte Carlo simulation with a variability of returns, or (3) input your own rate of return.

If you enter your own rate of return into the financial planning software, keep in mind that the higher the number, the lower your chances of accomplishing your goals, requiring larger adjustments to your financial plan down the road.

If you default to the software's preset growth rate in your retirement projections, that number is not always readily displayed within a 40-page printout. For you to have confidence in staying on track with your financial plan, it is essential that you have clarity about the preset growth rate used in the software.

For example, 10 years ago, Mark called me, wanting to compare the financial plan we had created together with the financial plan he had created for himself using an online calculator. Mark was 50 years old and wanted to retire as soon as possible but didn't want bad things to happen later in life, like drastically reducing his expenses to compensate for a flawed flight plan.

The financial plan we created together showed that he could retire at 62. The online calculator revealed he could retire at 55, and he wanted to know what was going on.

The sleuthing required to uncover the portfolio growth rate used by his online calculator amused both of us; it was buried deep in the 40-page document. We finally discovered that the online calculator relied on historical rates of return on stocks and bonds, generating a growth rate almost double the 4 percent we used in his original projection.

Mark can use a 7 percent growth rate or a 4 percent growth rate in his projections. He will just have to make bigger adjustments to his power settings along the way to stay on track if the expectations he has in his financial plan don't match up with the reality that unfolds.

Some financial plans and many financial planners integrate a Monte Carlo analysis to simulate a wide range of outcomes for your portfolio. There is nothing wrong with its analysis, but there is nothing special about a Monte Carlo tool.

If, after looking at the myriad of outputs generated by a Monte Carlo analysis, you conclude that it is Wall Street and Academia's attempt at making your retirement planning efforts more complicated than they need to be, you are not alone.

Monte Carlo simulations generate a probability of the success of your financial plan: the sustainability of your portfolio over your lifetime. Monte Carlo simulations require you to fly the same flight plan as investors who shun Monte Carlo simulations . . .

. . . dial in your power settings and make small adjustments along the way.

Let's look at this concept of making small adjustments along the way as it relates to the return expectations you have for your portfolio.

If you project common stocks to generate a 7 percent annualized return (nominal) and investment-grade corporate bonds to return 2 percent over the next 10 years,[1] depending on your allocation between stocks and bonds, a projected growth rate of 3, 4, or 5 percent would be a logical input to your financial plan.

Whether you use 3, 4, or 5 percent in your projection isn't as important as the small adjustments you make each year based on

[1]Vanguard Market perspectives (June 2020). 10-year annualized return projections for US equities is 5.5–7.5 percent, global equities (ex-US) 8.5–10.5 percent, US credit bonds 1.8–2.8 percent.

what unfolds in your life and what unfolds in the stock market and bond market.

The same is true for the power setting of inflation in your financial plan. It is convenient to use the calculator's default inflation rate generated by the Consumer Price Index (CPI); however, the inflation rate that counts is your personal inflation rate, not the CPI. In other words, how much are your expenses increasing each year? The only way you will know is if you keep track of your expenses – a simple concept for a life of wealth and happiness.

You might have monthly expenses in retirement of $8,000 that increase 1 percent yearly over the next 20 years, while your recently retired neighbor might have the same expenses that climb 3 percent a year. This variance will have a massive impact on the sustainability of your portfolio.

Working with Coffeehouse Investors over the past 20 years, I have observed the effect of a personal inflation rate. Addressing this power setting acknowledges that you have created an awareness of how money flows through your life, and the financial harmony that results from this clarity.

Am I on track? Dial in your power settings and make small adjustments along the way.

Once you have your power settings dialed in, you can move on to the juicy part of your financial plan – your allocation between stocks and bonds. In 1983, when I started working at Smith Barney, AA-rated municipal bonds yielded 9 percent, interest rates on three-month certificates of deposit (CDs) were 15 percent, and inflation the previous five years had been running at 8.5 percent.

Now, one-year CDs are yielding about 1 percent, which makes for a challenging financial plan if you choose to invest your entire portfolio in 1 percent CDs. The allocation you choose between stocks and bonds is essential to the sustainability of your portfolio. What is the right allocation for you?

For starters, how about keeping any money you might need from your portfolio over the next 10 years out of the stock market, placed in something less volatile, like CDs or bonds? That way, you probably won't have to sell your common stock investments at a loss to pay your bills. This will allow you to periodically sell stocks at a gain during the next bull market to rebalance your portfolio.

Whether you keep 5 years or 15 years of expenses out of the stock market depends as much on your emotional ability as your financial ability to withstand bear markets in common stocks.

Selling your common stocks at a loss to pay your bills greatly reduces the sustainability of your portfolio, a concept known as "sequence of returns" risk. With current yields on bonds so low and the sequence of returns risk so high, creating a smart asset allocation for your flight plan is essential, especially during the years immediately after you retire from earned income.

Now, let's discuss everyone's favorite question: What do you think about the 4 percent rule?

When you start withdrawing money from your portfolio to pay bills in retirement, what is a safe withdrawal rate so that you never run out of money? In the world of Wall Street and Academia, this question will be debated forever.

Apparently, somebody came up with the idea that if you withdraw 4 percent of your portfolio in retirement, you will never run out of money. The thing about the 4 percent rule is that it pretty much ignores all your power settings. The 4 percent safe withdrawal rate is debated as if it is a static decision never to be changed throughout one's lifetime. It is like suggesting to me that once I get on the glide slope to descend into Boeing Field, I can't make any adjustments along the way.

Bad things will happen. At least that's what they told me in flight school.

Today, Wall Street and Academia argue that the safe withdrawal rate is now 2 percent, or 3 percent, or should remain at 4 percent. The irony of this debate is that it does not matter. Dial in your power settings, figure out a withdrawal *amount* that makes sense for you based on your financial plan, and make small adjustments along the way. Some of you will want to sustain the entire principal of your portfolio over your lifetime. Most of you will need to draw down at least a portion of your principal throughout your lifetime. To each their own. Dial in your power settings and make small adjustments along the way.

Am I on track?

I connected with a couple I'll call John and Carrie 19 years ago when they were in their early fifties. They had been reading my column in the local paper and were fixated on the stock market, but only because their stockbroker was fixated on the stock market. They reached out to me with one burning question.

Are we on track to retire in 10 years?

To their credit, John and Carrie already had their saving and spending dialed in. They knew how much they were spending and they knew how much they were saving. They wanted to retire in 10 years with a lifestyle comparable to the one they were living that day.

That sounds familiar.

Like most Coffeehouse Investors, it didn't take long for them to grasp the wisdom of owning a portfolio of index funds for a lifetime of investing. Even so, I reminded John and Carrie that although they might not be following the stock market much anymore, a portion of their portfolio will still be invested in common stocks, and to plan on many more bear markets throughout their lifetime.

That's the stock market for you. Two steps forward and one step back.

It is easy to talk about the stock market in a theoretical manner of two steps forward and one step back. In real life, the two steps forward can last two years or 20 years. One step back can last more than three years or less than three weeks.

Everyone wants to talk about the stock market when new technologies are spurring new industries driven by new ideas, corporate earnings are increasing, employment is dropping, and the stock market is generating annual returns of 10, 20, or 30 percent a year.

It isn't so easy embracing the inevitable bear markets, even though in our financial planning we have planned for just that.

One step back.

I have lived through lots of bear markets during the past 40 years, and when the one step back in a financial plan becomes the one step back in reality, we deal with a whole different set of emotions.

Will it come back?

The 1987 stock market crash made us wonder, will it come back?

The dot-com bubble bursting and the 9/11 terrorist attack made us wonder, will it come back?

The 2008 financial crisis made us wonder, will it come back?

The 2020 COVID-19 pandemic makes us wonder, will it come back?

As long as we are invested in common stocks, we will wonder. Will it come back? Either it will or it won't. If it does come back, the stock market will eventually move to new heights, because it reflects the relentless productivity of human beings around the globe. If it doesn't come back, and global productivity grinds to a halt, well, the money you have stored safely away in CDs won't be worth the FDIC insurance backing it.

I am not suggesting that you should blindly allocate a portion of your portfolio to common stocks. I know many Coffeehouse Investors who have their entire portfolio in CDs or bonds, because they have created a financial plan that works for them.

Once you settle in on an asset allocation that works for you, it is time to begin focusing on other components of your financial plan, like:

- Your rainy-day fund
- Estate planning
- Roth conversions

- Asset location
- Asset allocation
- Insurance planning
- Retirement planning
- Tax-efficient accumulation strategies
- Tax-efficient withdrawal strategies
- Mortgage payoffs
- Healthcare planning
- Educational funding
- Tax planning
- Charitable planning
- Eldercare planning
- Social Security analysis
- Immediate annuities analysis
- Reverse mortgages

These are some of the issues John and Carrie will address over a lifetime of financial planning, just to name a few. I suspect you might need to address a few of them over your lifetime as well.

John and Carrie created a financial plan toward the end of 2001. As the bear market in common stocks continued to unfold into 2002, I called to check in. Their response was "Hey Bill, we won't be drawing any money from our portfolio for the next 10 years, so we aren't much concerned about the decline."

John and Carrie updated their financial plan each year to include updated power settings, making little adjustments along the way.

In early 2009, as they were approaching retirement and the stock market was plummeting, I called to check in. Their response was,

"Hey Bill, we've got the next 10 years of expenses outside the stock market, so we aren't much concerned about the decline."

John and Carrie continued to update their financial plan each year based on their power settings, making little adjustments along the way to reflect what was unfolding in their lives and unfolding in the markets.

In early 2020, when the stock market was down 33 percent, I called them to check in, and you know what their response was? "Hey Bill, we've got the next 10 years of expenses outside of the stock market, so we aren't much concerned about the decline." We discussed the possibility that the stock market could decline another 30 percent over the next three months, and stay down for three years, like it did in early 2000. Their response was the same.

Although they have a healthy allocation in common stocks, John and Carrie live their lives as if the stock market doesn't exist. They realize bear markets are a fact of life. They understand bear markets in common stocks are integral to the functioning of capital markets.

Over a lifetime of investing, you are likely to endure a bear market every six to eight years.[2] Now, you can endure bear markets because you have planned for bear markets in your financial plan.

If you are not prepared emotionally and financially for the next bear market, you are likely to get fixated on the stock market and the performance of your portfolio, because that is what Wall Street and everyone else seems to fixate on. One of the dangers

---

[2]Source: Capital Group.

of fixating on the stock market is that you begin to focus on something that is out of your control, instead of everything that *is* in your control.

Fixating on one thing, especially on one thing that is out of your control will get you in trouble. At least that is what they told me in flight school.

Every flight instructor drilled in to me the danger of fixating on one instrument, especially while descending on the glide slope in the clouds. Bad things will happen.

Keep the eye scan going: airspeed indicator, attitude indicator, vertical speed indicator, glide scope, localizer, pitch, power, trim, airspeed indicator, attitude indicator, vertical speed indicator, glide scope, localizer, pitch, power, trim.

All the way down.

When it comes to creating a financial plan, getting on track and staying on track can have a profoundly positive impact on *your* attitude indicator. I know it does on mine. That "on-track" feeling with my financial plan spills into all areas of my life, like maintaining a stable descent into Boeing Field.

When I was a kid on the farm, I didn't know anything about glide slopes and attitude indicators. My brother and I built airplanes out of plywood and 2-by-4s. Today, I don't care if it's a Citation or a two-seater Cessna flying overhead, I stop and look up and marvel at this thing called flight.

We moved on to rubber band–powered airplanes, and then started making balsa airplanes fueled by gas-powered Cox engines. When my brother was 17, we built his ultralight airplane in our farm shop. If you want to know how that turned out, read my first book.

A few years later, I moved to Illinois to work at the Chicago Board of Trade. I spent my Saturday mornings lying on my back at the end of Chicago's O'Hare airport, watching jumbo airliners departing and landing overhead.

My brother made a career out of flying for the airlines, while I chose a career in financial services. There have been times that I wished I had followed in my brother's footsteps, but now I would not change a thing. I am the luckiest person in the world because I get to work on both financial plans *and* flight plans.

Six years ago I signed up for an introductory flight out of Boeing Field, just south of downtown Seattle. The pilot took me for a short flight around Puget Sound and let me fly the airplane. Returning to Boeing Field, we banked hard right over the I-5 freeway to land on the short runway, with Air Traffic Control alerting us:

> *Caution, wake turbulence, Boeing 767 heavy landing on parallel runway.*

Commercial airliners from SEA-TAC International Airport were departing overhead. My palms were sweaty and I loved it.

I enrolled in a weekend flight training program, passed the oral exam, but failed the FAA check ride. I practiced my deficiencies and passed the check ride. I was a private pilot.

The fun part of getting your pilot's license around Seattle is that on a clear day, depending on which way you depart Boeing Field, in about 10 minutes you can see the San Juan Islands, Vancouver Island, and the Canadian Rockies to the north; Mt. Rainier, Mt.

St. Helen's, and Mt. Hood to the south; the Cascade Mountains to the east; and the Olympic mountains to the west. Below you is heaven, otherwise known as Puget Sound.

The not-so-fun part of flying around Seattle is that it is usually cloudy and rainy. If you want to fly much, you need your instrument flight rating (IFR), and so, at age 56, I set out to get my instrument flight rating so I could fly in the clouds.

There is an old saying, "You can't teach old dog new tricks," and maybe that's true. But, if you go through enough teachers, like Nicole, Natalie, Mark, and David, and the dog is really persistent, that kid off the farm has a chance to realize his dreams.

Dial in your power settings for a life of wealth and happiness.

I enrolled in a weekend IFR flight program, passed the oral exam, but failed the FAA check ride. I practiced my deficiencies and passed.

Today I am a private pilot with an IFR designation and my palms still get sweaty when I land at Boeing Field.

Now I have an excuse; I am descending through the clouds and I get to land on the big runway.

It is a long journey from building wooden airplanes on the farm to creating a financial plan and living a life of wealth and happiness.

But you have to start somewhere.

Use an online retirement calculator from Vanguard, Fidelity, Charles Schwab, or any of the financial planning software tools available online. Use an Excel spreadsheet. Use a yellow legal pad or the back of an envelope. Just start. Dial in your power settings. Make small adjustments along the way. Do it again next year, and the year after that.

I've never made a perfect landing, and you will never create the perfect financial plan, because it doesn't exist. However, the plan you create will reflect the life you want to live, and that is what I want to explore next.

7

Our Essential Creativity

We are swirling around in the Milky Way galaxy of our universe. We are not sure how we got here or where we are going, but I am quite sure there is an energy called life flowing through us all. The more we tap into this Energy of the Universe and cultivate our essential creativity, the more we will be able to live a life of wealth and happiness.

The most exciting part of this journey is that as we become our best selves, we nudge the global community to get in sync with the unfolding of the universe. We will talk more about working together to move things forward in the next chapter. For now, let's explore our own essential creativity in this pursuit.

Everyone has their own definition of a rich life. You know it when you are living it and confirm it when you see others living that same rich experience.

Deep in our bones we all have the desire to create: to imagine something new and bring that idea to life. A life of wealth and happiness materializes for me when my essential creativity comes alive. Connecting with Coffeehouse Investors over the years has confirmed my definition of a rich life.

I met Bob in 1983 when I moved to Seattle and my mother suggested that I get involved in the community. Bob is the father of one of the girls I coached on the youth volleyball team. At the time, Bob headed up Hospice of Seattle, and invited me to join the board of the organization. He went on to serve as CEO of a continuing care retirement center, nudging the global community to reimagine what it means to age with grace and dignity.

Tuning in to the Energy of the Universe, a process of slowing your life down enough to listen to that little voice inside and let it guide us, allows Bob to live a more fulfilling life and make a difference in the world. If you were to ask him how he tunes in to that energy, he would say it is simply living in the moment: being present to that which is in front of him today.

Don't spend too much time worrying about the past. Don't spend too much time worrying over the future. Live in the moment. That is the way Bob and his wife Julie live their lives. That is the way they manage their finances. I recall one of Bob's favorite quotes from Mark Twain, who said:

> *I have had a lot of worries in my life, most of which never happened.*

In other words, staying in the present is a helpful way to live, cultivating a focus on the here and now and avoiding unnecessary concerns about the future.

About 10 years before he retired, Bob wanted to confirm that he was on track with his financial plan, a one-page plan that listed his expected expenses and income in retirement. Bob is not one to be impressed with Wall Street things like standard deviations, Sharpe ratios, Monte Carlo simulations, and the like. He simply wanted to confirm: "How much can I draw from my portfolio each year, so that it sustains me throughout my lifetime?"

- Save
- Invest
- Plan

Bob and Julie intuitively embraced the Coffeehouse ground rules long before I created the Coffeehouse Investor. Bob does not have the desire to keep up with what is going on in the stock market each day. He moves forward in his life knowing he is not missing out on a thing by the way he manages his investments and, more importantly, lives his life. Bob and Julie have created a harmony with the way money flows through their lives. Instead of the anxiety that arises from household money issues and the unknowns of the future, they use their financial resources to support a greater purpose within themselves and the global community.

That is a life of wealth and happiness.

Living in the moment and creating harmony with your money can be a turbulent journey. I have seen this struggle in others, and I have experienced it myself.

When I decided to quit my career as a stockbroker, I had to figure out a way to reduce my monthly spending by 90 percent. I had to live on $700 a month to make my money last for two years, before going back to work. For the first few months I was miserable. I probably would have stayed miserable had I not met Alexis, a spiritual counselor, who invited me to slow down my life, live in the moment, and discover my essential creativity.

Out of that discovery, I created the Coffeehouse Investor and started writing the newspaper column that led to my current career in financial planning.

Looking back on that experience of aligning my financial resources with my essential creativity, I do not want to portray it as some carefree journey of self-exploration. It was a gut-wrenching experience trying to figure out my next steps in life while living on $700 a month.

For every Coffeehouse Investor who embraces a life of wealth and happiness, there is someone who struggles to find a harmony with how money flows through their lives. It does not matter how much money you have, if you are a recent college grad, or someone nearing retirement.

It can happen to the best of us.

Not being in harmony with your money is illustrated by the story of Linda, who contacted me a while back to discuss her retirement. At 68 years old, she had recently endured the painful loss of her husband. She was intent on moving forward in this new chapter in her life, but emotionally paralyzed about her next steps.

In our conversations over the next few months, she told me that it was difficult for her to talk about money because her husband had always handled their finances. Her biggest fear was that she would not have enough money throughout her retirement and eventually become a financial burden on her children. This fear came from her experience growing up in a poor, single-parent household. Her fear of losing money in the stock market and running out of money later in life inhibited her taking the bold step of retiring.

Linda wanted to know the same thing as Bob: "How much can I draw from my portfolio each year and not run out of money?"

Linda went on to reveal the satisfaction she received in her career in healthcare administration. She acknowledged her anxiety of ending a job and facing the "emptiness of retirement," as she described it.

Linda's challenge is the challenge of many new retirees: listening to the Energy of the Universe as it guides you to stay connected to the global community and continue sharing your wisdom with the world. A key component to Linda's living in the moment will be her capacity to create harmony with money, so that she lives her retirement years with a spirit of abundance.

This got me to thinking. There are still *way* too many people like her, who have been financially prudent their entire lives, and still approach retirement with a scarcity mentality. Somehow, I need to do a better job tapping into my own essential creativity so that the work I do with *The Coffeehouse Investor* will reach *more* people like Linda who are yearning for that rich life they deserve.

When I set out to create *The Coffeehouse Investor* my primary mission was to introduce the simple concept of index funds to you. That was Round One of *The Coffeehouse Investor*.

Twenty years later, Coffeehouse Investors have revealed to me that index funds are only one small element of a life of wealth and happiness. What matters most is living in the moment, creating harmony with money (also known as living within your means), embracing a life of abundance, and making a difference in this world.

Round Two of *The Coffeehouse Investor* is to take these things that matter most, our ground rules for life, and share them in such a way that a seismic shift takes place in the way people save, invest, and live their lives.

And impact the world.

To make this happen, I need to continue exploring my essential creativity.

Over a quarter century ago, in a little town called La Conner, I had the blessing of slowing my life down enough to live in the moment, dig in the dirt, and create *The Coffeehouse Investor*.

My greatest challenge today, is to slow my life down in the swirling city of Seattle to live in the moment, dig in the dirt, and create Round Two.

Round Two starts by celebrating my daily rituals. This is nothing more than honoring the mundane things I do throughout the day. The more I celebrate my rituals, the more I live in the moment and tune in to the Energy of the Universe.

Elisabeth Kübler-Ross, a pioneer in embracing the hospice experience, said:

> *Learn to get in touch with the silence within yourself, and know that everything in life has purpose. There are no mistakes, no coincidences, all events are blessings given to us to learn from.*

A good place to begin creating ritual in your lives is to recognize the mundane routines that are a part of your day and then turn them into rituals. You wake up. That can become your first ritual. You make your bed. What kind of ritual can you make out of that? What do you do next? Your movement through the day presents opportunities for rituals that can be celebrated again and again. You begin to live in the moment.

Slowing your life down to identify your rituals is a healthy first step in tuning in to the Energy of the Universe and discovering your essential creativity.

My morning ritual after waking up, even when it is dark or raining outside, is to walk to the window and proclaim, "Good morning Mr. Sun, I'm glad I'm alive!" This ritual has a special meaning because it continues the ritual started out on the farm. When the sun came up over the hill and shone onto our kitchen table my father would proclaim:

"Good morning Mr. Sun, I'm glad I'm alive!"

Part of the messiness of my life has been the emptiness of trying to connect with my father over the years. This ritual gives me the opportunity to honor my father's life. Life unfolds as it should, and my father played a significant role in who I am today. The ritual is a chance to celebrate all the good stuff he *did* share with me.

My morning ritual continues with my favorite 10 minutes of the day. I close my eyes and hike up Mt. Rainier on the Muir snowfield. The hike, from the Paradise parking lot at 5,500 feet to the huts at Camp Muir about 5,000 feet higher, is just about the most beautiful hike in the world – especially if you are on the first leg of climbing that grand peak. This portion of the climb usually takes me about five hours if I am hauling a 40-pound backpack, and for the first couple of hours my mind is racing, stewing, fretting, worrying, and wondering. By the third hour, my mind starts to slow down as reality sets in. I am exhausted and I still have another two hours to climb.

I discovered early on in mountain climbing that the only way I can push on when total exhaustion sets in is to just take another 25 steps. If my mind is racing, stewing, fretting, worrying, and wondering, I will never make it another 25 steps. I am forced to think about nothing but the next 25 steps.

The reason I keep it at 25 steps is because that is all my mind can handle. Somewhere in the middle of that next two hours and 25 steps, I begin to experience the bliss of living in the moment.

That is the mental place I aim for with my morning meditation and it helps get me through my day.

I am happy going for long periods of time in complete silence. When I was a kid working on the farm, it was easy to daydream. Sitting on an old crawler tractor without a cab and without a radio, wearing goggles and a face mask to keep the dirt out, I could daydream all day long.

It is not so easy to daydream today, with family and work, and with easy access to every electronic gadget in my bag. I need to make my daily rituals count.

Round Two has arrived. I am ready and I am inspired by the legacy of John Bogle to press on.

I often wonder if he embraced rituals in his life, because he certainly lived in the moment. When my original manuscript was completed, Suzanne, my editor, suggested that I send him a draft, thanking him for his inspiration.

A few weeks later, I received a handwritten note from him, that read,

> *It is a wonderful book. Indeed, I am tempted to say, it looks like I wrote it myself. Now, if people will not only read Coffeehouse, but act on its message.*

Mr. Bogle was a towering legend in the financial services industry, and amid his busy life, took the time to respond to me. I wrote back to him, asking if I could use his comments as a blurb on the jacket of my new book.

He responded:

> *I'm delighted to participate vicariously in your well-deserved success. Press on.*

After the book was published, with Mr. Bogle's blurb on the cover, I sent him a copy, and he wrote back, commenting on the "missionary zeal" we all share in pushing forward to highlight Vanguard's mission.

A couple of years later in an interview with *Time* magazine, Mr. Bogle highlighted *The Coffeehouse Investor* as his top book for beginning investors. I sent him a thank-you card, and again he responded with a handwritten note, thanking me for my "discipleship in the index mission."

I am sure he received notes from investors all over the world, and I wouldn't be surprised if he responded to all of them

That is living in the moment.

We are invited to live in the moment with the same zeal as John Bogle. I wish I had some magical methods to make it happen for you, but I don't. All I can share is what has worked for me and what I have observed in others.

When I look around, there is an explosion of essential creativity unfolding in the global community, especially among young Coffeehouse Investors.

I had dinner a while back with some friends, including their two children, who invited several college-age friends over for the evening.

As the evening wore on, I was mesmerized listening to the career aspirations of these young adults. Later in the evening two guys at the dinner table turned to me and asked me about trading options; they had their eye on Netflix stock. We had a good laugh, but their question needs to be addressed from a Coffeehouse perspective. How can our younger investors start building financial wealth while settling into careers?

With commission-free trades and online trading accounts, too many young investors get caught up thinking they can build wealth by trading stocks and options and commodities and Bitcoin and anything else that catches their wealth-building attention.

The way I see it, the sadness is not that these aspiring traders will likely fail miserably at trading securities. The sadness is that they could be directing their essential creativity to building a lifetime of financial wealth.

If you are intent on building up your financial wealth early on, here are three tips from the Coffeehouse. They worked for me, they work for Coffeehouse Investors, and they can work for you.

1. *Save more.* No surprise here. It is the wisdom of *The Millionaire Next Door*, it was the wisdom of my municipal bond clients, and it is the wisdom of Coffeehouse Investors. Over the past 20 years I have seen the astounding impact of a consistent saving strategy for those who were 20 and are now 40 years old, and the 40-year-old who is now 60.

2. *Up your career* and save at least a portion of your increased earnings. The real benefit of upping your career is not necessarily in the additional savings; it is in your life, and in taking your essential creativity to the next level. With the vast array of online learning and advanced degrees now available, there is little excuse for you not to make this happen in your life.

3. *Start a business.* This is not a flippant suggestion. Start a business. The first step in starting a business is to start thinking about the business you want to start. It redirects your mental energy away from thinking you will get rich trading options and toward something that might allow you to build your financial wealth.

    It might take you two years to come up with your business idea, two more years to put the pieces together, and the next two years to get it up and running. Statistically, it will probably fail. So what? Start a second business. Statistically, your second startup has a greater chance of succeeding because you learned from your failed startup.

    Starting a business does not mean you need to quit your day job. It does mean you will need to draw on your essential creativity to make it happen. And it can happen. Look around you. Talk to a business owner in your neighborhood and find out what worked for them. Look at the needs of the world; look at the resources available at your fingertips to create a business to fill those needs. Turn off your electronics and start daydreaming.

When I was creating *The Coffeehouse Investor* over 25 years ago, access to the Internet was unfolding. I was trying to figure out the Internet, and a little voice inside me, affectionately called the Energy of the Universe, said I needed to create a website for my work. I purchased Microsoft's Frontpage web-building software, signed up for a web-building class, and built my own website. A few years later I started posting my weekly Coffeehouse Investor columns on the website, and it was probably one of the earlier financial blogs, around the time blogs were unfolding across the Internet.

Andrea, the coordinator of the web-building class, suggested I teach a Coffeehouse Investor class – so I did. Andrea believes in applying her essential creativity to the needs of the world. So as my class took off, I suggested to *her* that she launch her own company, focused on lifelong learning in the corporate arena. Inspired, Andrea started her own speaker's bureau serving Fortune 500 companies, nonprofits, and trade associations across North America.

Now, she's broadening her expertise by becoming a speaker herself. The topic? How and why to write what she calls Gracenotes®, also known as eulogies for the living. After all, we all want to know we *matter* – that we're making a difference in the world – *before* we pass.

Now it is Round Two of *The Coffeehouse Investor*.

Last year I decided to up my game. The Energy of the Universe was nudging me forward. I wanted to share what I had learned in the 20 years since writing *The Coffeehouse Investor*. I wanted to get the Coffeehouse ground rules into the hands and minds of more investors who want to live a life of wealth and happiness and make a difference in the world.

I needed help. I decided to hire a business coach and ran an online search, typing in "Top Business Coach in Seattle," and up popped Lisa.

Her website says it all:

> *Business Coaching for Values-Driven Entrepreneurs Who Dream of Changing the World – This is Your Time to Step Up & Make Your Difference*

Lisa's gift to the global community is rooted in her essential creativity, but her website did not pop up overnight. Her business started much the same as mine.

She had worked in the corporate and then the nonprofit worlds and realized these organizations didn't always have values similar to her own. The Energy of the Universe was talking to her. She didn't realize it at the time but her last job was the nudge forward to her new career as a business and leadership coach. It all unfolded two weeks before 9/11.

She used this time to dig in the dirt. She went back to school. Her passion was helping others discover their own purpose, working in organizations with aligned values. She started her business. Her first clients were her old co-workers.

Her business now thrives because she tunes in to her essential creativity and helps her clients tune into theirs. She succeeds because she has mastered that long-lost business skill of listening, and nudges her clients forward with her conversations about who they are and what they want to do with their life.

What do you really want from your life? What business are you daydreaming about? Who are you sharing it with today? What is the next step?

I could share lots of stories of Coffeehouse Investors who are using their essential creativity to build financial wealth as well as emotional, physical, and spiritual wealth. However, the story I want to share is of the greatest Coffeehouse Investor of them all – my mother.

Like all of us, buried in her bones is a desire to create, to bring ideas to life. As she lives her retirement years, she continues to nudge the global community forward with her quiet presence on that farmhouse overlooking the Snake River canyon.

I see my mother's life reflected in the lives of Coffeehouse Investors who take time to tune in to their children, and to their children's children, nudging *them* along to discover their essential creativity and make the world a better place.

When I visit my mother now, every morning we celebrate the sunrise, and in the evenings, we celebrate the sunset. When it turns dark, we go outside and gaze up at the stars in the night sky. On clear nights, when the moon isn't showing its face and it is pitch-black, we look up at the Milky Way galaxy in awe of the creation.

Sometimes my mother and I talk about her years growing up in Santa Monica, California, or her high school years in Spokane, Washington, or her calling to join a religious community. In her third year as a novitiate at Holy Cross in South Bend, Indiana, the Energy of the Universe nudged her to become a mother instead of a nun. She tells me of confiding her daydreams to a friend, who helped her get on a train back to Spokane, Washington. While she might call this moment in her life "listening to the voice of God," I call it "tuning in to the Energy of the Universe," and you can call it whatever you want. It doesn't really matter. We can all look up to the Milky Way galaxy and be in awe of creation.

Within three weeks of returning to the Northwest, she met my father, they got married, and together they created eight children.

My mother and father had a complicated relationship, but through it all she maintained a deep connection to her God. Somehow, the little girl who grew up near Beverly Hills, California, was now raising a family of eight on a farm overlooking the Snake River. It wasn't always fun, but she was good at living in the moment.

Through the years, she celebrated the lives of everyone in that little town, even when that town didn't always celebrate an outsider from Beverly Hills. She was there for the marriages and she was there for the divorces. She held the hands of neighbors who were having babies. She held the hands of neighbors who were dying, including the hand of her dying father-in-law after he took the life of his wife, his son, and, finally, his own.

After raising her own children, she helped raise the children of other families at her daycare business, Grandma Annie's, in that same little town.

Her essential creativity is expressed in her caring and kindness. She channels the Energy of the Universe through her own life into the lives of others with smallest of things, like the cards she sends and the phone calls she makes, that brighten the days of everyone.

I am sharing her story with you because her story should be everyone's story. Wealth and happiness come from the connections we build with each other, from the essential creativity that evolves with sharing and listening, and from knowing that your harmony with money you pass on to future generations will help them live their rich lives, just as you are living your rich life today.

It's time to take our essential creativity and nudge humanity forward.

8

Conversation Over Coffee

When we have arrived at the question, the answer is already near.
— Ralph Waldo Emerson

The conversations I have with Coffeehouse Investors usually move beyond financial things as we explore the planet's broader array of questions. In doing so, we nudge the global community forward.

That's why the financial conversations you have with yourself, your partner, and your household are essential. Money has a way of creating anxiety when there isn't harmony in the way it flows into and out of our lives. It doesn't matter how much you make or how much you spend. If money creates anxiety, it saps your energy.

We need your essential creativity. We need that part of you that wants to touch people's lives, not because you want to save the world, but because touching people's lives and making a difference gives you joy and hope and happiness.

That is the Energy of the Universe for me.

We are at a crossroads in our journey, accelerated by the COVID-19 pandemic. When we look beyond the darkness of the moment, across the horizon of humanity, the universe is unfolding as it should. This past year we are reminded that we are closely connected and that the choices we make matter to those around us and beyond. Let's take advantage of this moment and through our connections and conversations discover new ways to shine our lives and light on the world.

There are some basic, universal laws that you have probably gotten reacquainted with this past year, like eating healthy, exercising, and living in the moment. I am guessing you also reviewed the financial harmony in your life, carefully examining how you save and spend money. Initiating financial conversations allows you to move on to life's deeper conversations: you know, the conversations that get started early in the morning with that first cup of coffee and carry on into the night.

The Energy of the Universe has been conversing with me my whole life, even though, at times, I have tuned it out. I have come to a point in my life where I now realize the conversations I have with you and the conversations I have with the Energy of the Universe are the same thing.

The first chapter of this book started off with an e-mail I received from Gene. He shared a conversation with his family and friends, introducing the Coffeehouse ground rules to them. Gene is changing the world, one investor at a time.

The conversation Gene had with his family and friends might not have taken place had I never had a conversation with my mother, who encouraged me to get involved with my community.

At her nudging, I signed up to coach a youth volleyball team and met a dad named Bob. Ten years later, in a conversation I had with him, he invited me to volunteer with Hospice of Seattle. Hospice nudged me to quit my job at Smith Barney and pursue a richer life.

This search led me to meeting Alexis while on a bike ride to Portland, Oregon. It was Alexis who told me to go dig in the dirt and figure out my life.

The way I look at it, because of the conversations I had with my mother, Bob, and Alexis, the family and friends of Gene are now set to nudge the world forward; the financial harmony they create in their lives allows them to share their essential creativity with the world.

A few years ago, my brother reached out to me and said, "Hey Bill, you've got to read a book called *Factfulness* by Hans Rosling,"[1] so I bought a copy. Its message confirmed what I have felt all along: the world is getting better, not worse. It is messy, but it is getting better. You might argue against the book's premise and that's okay; that is part of the conversation. Sometimes it's hard to recognize this progress, because the incremental change that is evolving rarely makes the daily news reports.

The world is messy.

---

[1]Rosling, Hans, with Ola Rosling and Anna Rosling Ronnlund. (2018). *Factfulness: Ten Reasons We're Wrong About the World – and Why Things Are Better Than You Think*. New York: Flatiron Books.

The world is getting better.

Reading *Factfulness* touched me at my core because its message is integral to the ground rules of Coffeehouse Investors. The global community is relentless in moving forward and we are counting on the long-term returns of global stock markets to reflect this collective productivity. How we view the world plays an essential role, not only in how we invest our money, but in how our children, and our children's children, view the world and live their lives.

If we are hopeless, they will feel hopeless. If we dwell on the negative, they are apt to dwell on the negative. If we have an optimistic view of things, that good energy will be passed down and inspire others to share their essential creativity. If we have harmony with our money, that will serve as an example for others to follow.

Factfulness's author Hans Rosling presents a simple thesis – that the world's population can be divided into four income levels:

> *Level 1 represents the population that struggles to find clean water, and that works all day just to eat a meal at night.*
> *Level 4 is the level you have likely attained if you are reading this book, with an income that provides for most of life's necessities.*
> *Levels 2 and 3 are a continuum from Level 1 to Level 4, as described in his book.*

According to Rosling, this is the population in each level:

Level 1: 1 billion people
Level 2: 3 billion people

Level 3: 2 billion people
Level 4: 1 billion people

Rosling describes the movement of human beings from level 1 to level 2, then to level 3, and finally to level 4. It is the great Energy of the Universe flowing through us, that inspires us to go to work every day – not just to survive, but to push forward for a better life. Through this process we share our good ideas – our essential creativity – with others. We improve our own lives, the lives of our families, and the lives of our global community.

A family wants to have access to clean water, but they don't stop there. They want access to nearby clean water. And then they want access to clean water in their home, and then hot water for showers. The pursuit of a better life will never stop.

One question that continues to come up in conversations with the global community, and will continue to challenge our essential creativity, is, "How can the global community continue to move to the next level with our finite resources, without tipping the scales?"

Another question that challenges our essential creativity is, "When you reach level 4, and have everything you need materially, how do you honor that part of your DNA that will forever yearn for more?" It seems to me that the challenge is to turn this pursuit of "more" away from material consumption and toward a "more" that fosters more family, more community, more connections, more art, more creativity, more beauty, more people wanting to work for more businesses that are in sync with Rosling's message.

Rosling points out that progress results from the sharing of ideas in an economic and political system that *allows* good ideas to come to life in the marketplace of capitalism.

That is a spicy conversation. How do we take this thing called capitalism and keep it a good thing, so that it continues to foster a better world? Addressing that question should be at the forefront of our essential creativity, and is starting to unfold across the investing landscape through the introduction of index funds that have a focus on sustainability.

In 1993 I rode my bike to Portland, stopping for the night at the halfway spot, when I met Alexis, who worked at a Jesuit Retreat House. She is the one who suggested I dig in the dirt to figure out my life. She also suggested that I read a book, *Original Blessing*, by Matthew Fox, a spiritual teacher and former Catholic, now Episcopal, priest.[2] Drawing on his essential creativity, he proposes a new way of looking at the global community.

I grew up in a traditional German Catholic community, where the idea of original sin was a core part of Catholic theology. I was taught that people are born bad, but, through the grace of God, they can become good. That idea of people being born bad never really made sense to me, and I wondered how this idea of original sin has played out in the global reach of religion over the centuries.

In *Original Blessing*, Fox presents a theology that might be more in line with the Energy of the Universe. We are born inherently blessed and infinitely valuable; and out of that infinitely valuable life spills a creative energy that nudges humanity forward.

For now, I want to highlight another book of his. In 1995 Fox wrote *The Reinvention of Work: A New Vision of Livelihood for Our*

---

[2]Fox, Matthew. (2000). *Original Blessing: A Primer in Creation Spirituality Presented in Four Paths, Twenty-Six Themes, and Two Questions*. Putnam.

Time.[3] Fox suggests that we will have to call on our essential creativity in the workplace for the global community to continue to prosper.

He writes,

> *It is not money but need that creates work. Right work will in turn create more work, provided we have answered questions of need correctly. What work is the universe asking of us at this time? What work is the Earth asking of us at this time? What work are the other species asking of us at this time? What work are the youth asking of us at this time? What work are the future generations of humans asking of us? What work are our hearts asking of us? We don't need just any kind of work or any kind of job at this moment in history. What we need is the right work for the right times.*

What is the work your heart is asking of you? Creating a space to celebrate your essential creativity is not only for weekend warriors who dabble in the arts. According to Fox, it is an everyday showing-up-for-work type of creativity that is necessary for you to thrive in your career.

In discussing this thing called essential creativity, it might sound like we are born to do great things like discover a vaccine or lead a company. It is so much more than that. It is being fully present in whatever you are doing, and doing it the best you can. It means pushing through your mundane job that doesn't necessarily provide you joy, but at least pays your bills. What can you do in the present moment that will allow you to be infinitely valuable to others? Perhaps it is in the way you are kind and considerate and thoughtful and interested in those around you.

---

[3]Fox, Matthew. (1995). *The Reinvention of Work: A New Vision of Livelihood for Our Time*. HarperCollins.

I love that long-ago Coca-Cola TV commercial with Bob Hope. He comes on the screen and says, "One little smile isn't going to change the world, but it's a nice place to start."

I love connecting with people who change the world with a smile. I remember taking the Metro Bus, Seattle's public transportation, to downtown Seattle every day. Each year Metro selected a "driver of the year." One time the driver of the year was a woman in her late fifties who drove my route. Every day I got on her bus she greeted me as if I were her most important passenger. She greeted every passenger that way. It wasn't long before that whole bus was energized by her early morning smile.

One day I asked her what inspires her. She said she meets such interesting people, and her riders have changed her life. She is one person who changed my life in the way I engage with people. She nudges the global community forward. She lives her essential creativity.

Finding that creativity can be a long and difficult journey.

Debby, a reader of my Coffeehouse Investor column, reached out to me about 13 years ago, looking to confirm the choices she had made within her workplace retirement account. Together, we mapped out a financial plan that would allow her to retire in 17 years.

When we connected again the following year to update the plan, she shared her frustration at working in a cyclical industry where every three years she was looking for a new job. I asked her what she was daydreaming about for a better job, and she didn't have much to say. We met again the following year to update her financial plan and again she shared her frustrations with her job. Again I asked her what she was daydreaming about, and she didn't have much to say.

The next year we met to update her financial plan and Debby told me about a dog-grooming business in her neighborhood that was about to shut down. All she could think about was owning her own dog-grooming business, because she loves dogs and she loves people. We discussed her staying in a dead-end career or quitting that job, getting a loan to buy the business, and, if the loan fell through, liquidating her retirement plan to cover the loan. We talked about the risk of purchasing the business, and we talked about the risk of remaining in her current job, where, in her own words, she felt "bored out of my mind."

She followed our meeting up with a phone call, told me she had been playing it safe for too long, and had decided to buy the dog-grooming business.

I kept an eye on Debby's business, and caught up with her this past year to see how she was holding up with the economic slowdown. We reflected on the conversation we had 13 years ago. I asked her what she had learned in growing her successful business. She said the same thing that Bob told me. "I've learned to live in the moment. I built my loyal customers by being fully present to everyone who walks through the door."

For Debby, her business came about because she decided to allow her essential creativity to move beyond a daydream; now she nudges the global community forward.

I am not suggesting you liquidate your retirement plan and purchase the next business that catches your eye. But with what we've endured this past year on the economic front, I can only imagine the thousands of closed storefronts across the United States waiting for the next Debby to show up, open up shop, and share their essential creativity with the world.

When we look at what has unfolded from COVID-19, the Energy of the Universe is virtually crying out for us to nurture our creativity.

We can create better educational systems.

We can create better systems for an aging population.

We can create better healthcare systems.

We can create healthier workplace environments.

We can create healthier food experiences.

We can create better recreational experiences.

We can create better tools for nurturing creativity in others.

We can create better ways to use energy.

We can create better dog-grooming businesses.

We can create simpler financial plans.

We can create smiles, and change the world.

These are just a few of the ideas that have come up in conversations with Coffeehouse Investors, who are looking beyond COVID-19 to nudge humanity along in the right direction.

Don't have any ideas of your own? Go dig in the dirt. Go for a long walk. I'm not talking about a walk around the block; I'm talking about a four-hour walk by yourself – without your phone, because leaving your phone behind gives you an opportunity to live in the moment and tune in to the Energy of the Universe where your essential creativity is stored.

Better yet, hike up to Camp Muir.

Recently I called my friend Tony, whom you met in Chapter 1, and asked how his life was treating him in the midst of the COVID-19 crisis. With the school year winding down, I could hear that huge smile on his face, as he paused for words. He finally said, "It is interestingly complex."

As the school's principal, I suspect there were times over the previous four months when all Tony wanted to say was "life's messy." Instead, with a smile, he says it is "interestingly complex." He is in the middle of reinventing this education thing on the fly. He said half the kids are engaged and the other half aren't. Half the parents are engaged, and the other half aren't. He said he gets his inspiration from everyone.

Long before COVID-19 showed up, Tony was set to embark on a four-year program to obtain his doctorate, with a focus on distance learning platforms.

And then life takes a turn, as it always does, and COVID-19 invites educators, parents, and students to take this distance learning platform to the next level. And why not? The Energy of the Universe asks all of us to do the same thing – to take our essential creativity to the next level and make this a better world.

Laurence Siegel, in his book *Fewer, Richer, Greener,*[4] writes about the same thing Tony is working on. According to Siegel, the first big equalizer in education resulted from the Gutenberg printing press around 1450. The second big equalizer was the public education system that unfolded in America and around the world beginning in the late nineteenth century. In his book, Siegel writes:

> *The Third Democratization of Education is being made possible by the Internet, and it is just getting started.*

Tony takes his work to the next level and he inspires me to take my work to the next level. Conversations with Coffeehouse Investors nudge all of us to take it to the next level in pursuit of wealth and happiness.

Knowing Tony, in another 25 years he'll probably be saying the same things David said in the e-mail I shared with you in Chapter 1:

> *I am a lucky man as I approach retirement. I have two healthy children, I am more in love with my wife than ever before, and I have made a few modest, but wise investments along the way. I wonder how many 55-year-old elementary school principals can say the same.*

Tony and Katie define wealth and happiness the same way Coffeehouse Investors define it: by expressing their essential creativity to make a difference. It is the same way you want your children, and your children's children, to define it, because you know it is a more authentic version of wealth and happiness than the definition promoted by Madison Avenue.

---

[4]Siegel, Laurence B. (2020). *Fewer, Richer, Greener: Prospects for Humanity in an Age of Abundance*. Hoboken, NJ: John Wiley & Sons.

For Tony and Katie, a life of wealth and happiness evolves from harmony in the way money flows through their lives. Harmony doesn't necessarily mean you are on track to reach your financial goals. Financial harmony begins with a conversation about getting on track: to pay your bills on time, to initiate a retirement account, to establish a rainy-day fund, to create a financial plan.

There will be obstacles and challenges along the way. Tony already knows that life is interestingly complex. He has discovered that the harmony you have with money makes the complex encounters of life more manageable.

Ralph Waldo Emerson said,

> *To know even one life has breathed easier because you have lived.*
> *This is to have succeeded.*

That is the spirit of Coffeehouse Investors, and that is our definition of success.

You have the same opportunity to create harmony in the way money flows through your life. Through the conversations and connections you have with your children and your children's children, a life will breathe easier because of you.

We are not finished. We are just getting started. I look at my own life, and I am just starting to tune in to my unlimited essential creativity and share it with you.

My goal is to share the Coffeehouse ground rules with everyone who accepts responsibility for their own financial independence in retirement. I know I will never reach my goal of "everyone," so I will be working on this as long as I can. The fun part is, the more I work on it, the more conversations I have with people like you, and the more I live a life of joy, hope, and happiness.

Life is messy – always has been, always will be. We can look at our country, we can look at our world, and say they are messy, and miserable, and getting worse. We can have the defeatist attitude that our actions don't matter, and so why even bother to try? Or, we can say that what we are doing is critically important, that our actions do matter, as life has shown us this past year, and we are nudging the world forward.

Mother Teresa, caretaker to the poor, said,

> *We ourselves feel that what we are doing is a drop in the ocean.*
> *But the ocean would be less because of that missing drop.*

Coffeehouse Investors make a difference, even if only a drop, in the lives they live, and reinforce my conviction that our ground rules are essential to a life of wealth and happiness.

You deserve to live your rich life.

The world needs you to make a difference.

Start with the ground rules.

Epilogue

This book evolved from a desire to tell my story. Ultimately, it isn't my story, it is your story. It is about you, and your desire to live a life of wealth and happiness by embracing simple ground rules. You are the one who has taken these ground rules and integrated them into your purpose-driven life. If it wasn't for you, there would be no story – there would be no Coffeehouse Investor.

When we look beyond the mountains of stuff that Wall Street throws our way, our financial needs are simple. "Can I live a meaningful life and still pay my bills?" That is a question many of us have wrestled with at one time or another, even when we are working.

"Can I pay my bills for the next 30 years when I'm not working?" takes on a whole new meaning when we contemplate retirement. Day after day, over the past 20 years, I have connected with Coffeehouse Investors who are retired, who do pay their bills and don't give it a second thought, because they have created a harmony with the way money flows through their lives.

Kudos to them. They achieved this harmony within a retirement system that is broken. It works for some, but not many. The system needs a restart. Someday we will have a system that works for everyone. This new system will allow everyone an opportunity to pay their bills during retirement with the money they save while working. Someday every worker will be offered the option of investing in a personal pension plan, much like the traditional defined benefit pension plan of years gone by, or Social Security today, except now, *you*, not your employer, are saving for your retirement pension.

Before we start exploring the benefits of a personal pension plan, let us look at why the system is broken, and where to go from here.

Prior to 401(k) plans taking hold in the early 1980s, company retirement programs consisted largely of private pensions, also known as defined benefit plans. For workers lucky enough to be employed at a company that offered these pension plans, the monthly pension check you received at retirement depended on a couple of factors, including how long you worked at the company and your salary during the last years of your working career.

Let's look at the traditional pension plan of a worker named Emily. As Emily's career unfolds, she calculates that she will receive a pension check of about $4,500/month at 65. On top of that, she starts getting updates from the Social Security office informing her that at the full retirement age of 66 her Social Security check will be about $3,500 per month.

Want to guess where Emily starts managing her lifestyle while working? By making sure that her monthly expenses in retirement are less than $8,000 per month.

If she wants anything beyond that, she knows she needs to save more while working, but at least Emily knows she has $8,000 in expenses covered each month.

She knows she can pay her bills in retirement and she doesn't have to deal with Wall Street and the stock market. Emily will never have to sit through a mind-numbing Monte Carlo analysis.

She doesn't care about "sequence of returns" risk. Factor Funds? Not for her. She ignores 40-page risk analyzer questionnaires. All she wants to do in her retirement is live a life of wealth and happiness – and pay her bills.

It was nice while it lasted.

In 1978 Congress passed the Tax Reform Act of 1978, and inserted paragraph "k" into section 401 of the Internal Revenue Code, allowing employees an opportunity to contribute pretax earnings into a workplace retirement account. The change in tax code was never meant to be a substitute for Emily's traditional pension plan. Its primary purpose was to allow top executives and highly compensated employees an opportunity to defer compensation, primarily from bonuses and stock options, within an employer-sponsored account.

Soon after the creation of the 401(k) plan, however, pension consultants started suggesting large employers take the opportunity to dramatically reduce costs by freezing traditional pension plans for current employees and encouraging both them and new employees to start contributing to the new 401(k) plan. From the employer's perspective, they shouldn't be responsible for Emily's retirement when she can do it herself.

This decision, to shift the retirement burden off the backs of employers and onto the backs of employees, was done without any thought. It just happened. It was a fluke. Workers did not have any say in it. There was no collaboration between employers, employees, financial institutions, and Congress to design a meaningful alternative to the traditional pension plans.

Sam pays the price. Sam is a new hire, and now Sam is responsible for deciding whether to save in the 401(k) plan, and how much to save. After deciding he wants to participate in the retirement plan, Sam must now decide how the money is to be invested among the lineup of available mutual funds. When Sam retires, the challenge begins. He has to figure out how much money to pull out of his account each month so that he doesn't run out of money before he dies. Sam spends three hours in front of his computer every morning for the first year of his retirement trying to learn about the 4 percent safe withdrawal rule, only to find out that by the time he fully understands it, the consensus has changed to 3 percent.

Let's compare the harmony of Emily, who owns a traditional pension, with the stress of Sam, who owns a 401(k) plan.

While working, Emily grows into a lifestyle knowing that when she retires, if she keeps her expenses below $8,000, she will be able to pay her bills. Sam, on the other hand, while saving during his career, has no idea how much he needs to save to eventually cover his evolving lifestyle in retirement.

It is preposterous to think that Sam, an average intelligent person, should be expected to successfully save enough money over a 40-year period of employment, making wise investment decisions along the way, and then, once retired, draw it down in an intelligent manner over a 25-year period of unemployment called retirement.

Enter Wall Street, which has been part of the problem, but can also be part of the solution.

With 401(k) plans flourishing in the early 1980s, mutual fund companies capitalized on this emerging phenomena by offering workers an array of mostly expensive mutual funds that generated exorbitant fees for the mutual fund companies. Employers gave lip service to employee financial education, but for the most part, Sam was on his own. It worked for a while, and it was nice while it lasted, at least while the stock market generated annualized returns of 18 percent.

Things have changed over the years, as workers have demanded more. Many 401(k) plans now include automatic enrollment options, target-date funds, and financial planning software to help employees like Sam answer the question, "How much do I need to save today to pay my expenses in retirement?"

That is the question every employee wants to know, and that is what financial institutions need to address: "How much do I need to save today to pay my expenses in retirement?" If workers like Sam could answer that question, it would have a deep impact on how much he saves today, and his quality of life throughout retirement.

Our country does have a savings problem. Part of the problem is that some people won't take responsibility for saving today for a secure future. Working with you over the past 20 years, I have found that there are many more who *do* want to save; you do want to take responsibility for a secure retirement. The problem is, in our current system, the whole saving and investing thing is so nebulous that many don't know where to start. And so they don't.

We are working together to fix a broken system, but it doesn't happen overnight. Auto enrollment has become the standard. Almost 35 years after John Bogle established Vanguard, target-date funds have become the default choice of many 401(k) plans. Creating a Coffeehouse Investor–type portfolio through a target-date fund is a good start, but it isn't enough. In December 2019, Congress passed the SECURE Act that includes opportunities for 401(k) plans to be converted into income streams at retirement, so that the money built up in a 401(k) can be converted to a self-funded pension. That has its own cautionary challenges, but it is a start.

In the meantime, you and I will continue working together, introducing to everyone the Coffeehouse Investor ground rules:

- Save
- Invest
- Plan

We can help each other move beyond this broken system as we pursue a life of wealth and happiness. It is a daunting challenge. We are up to the task.

Further Reading

Bernstein, William. (2014). *If You Can: How Millennials Can Get Rich Slowly*. Efficient Frontier Publications.

Bogle, John. (2019). *Stay the Course – The Story of Vanguard and the Index Revolution*. Hoboken, NJ: John Wiley & Sons.

Clear, James. (2018). *Atomic Habits: An Easy & Proven Way to Build Good Habits & Break Bad Ones*. New York: Penguin.

Foster, Richard, and Kaplan, Sarah. (2001). *Creative Destruction: Why Companies That Are Built to Last Underperform the Market – and How to Successfully Transform Them*. New York: Currency/Doubleday.

Fox, Matthew. (2000). *Original Blessing: A Primer in Creation Spirituality Presented in Four Paths, Twenty-Six Themes, and Two Questions*. New York: Putnam.

Gann, Ernest K. (1961). *Fate Is the Hunter – A Pilot's Memoir*. New York: Simon & Schuster.

Gawande, Atul. (2014). *Being Mortal: Medicine and What Matters in the End*. New York: Picador.

Larimore, Taylor. (2018). *The Boglehead's Guide to the Three-Fund Portfolio*. Hoboken, NJ: John Wiley & Sons.

Phau, Wade. (2019). *Safety-First Retirement Planning: An Integrated Approach for a Worry-Free Retirement*. Vienna, VA: Retirement Researcher Media.

Robin, Vicki, and Dominguez, Joe. (1992). *Your Money or Your Life: 9 Steps to Transforming Your Relationship with Money and Achieving Financial Independence*. New York: Penguin Books.

Rosling, Hans, with Ola Rosling and Anna Rosling Ronnlund. (2018). *Factfulness: Ten Reasons We're Wrong About the World – And Why Things Are Better Than You Think*. New York: Flatiron Books.

Siegel, Laurence B. (2020). *Fewer, Richer, Greener: Prospects for Humanity in an Age of Abundance*. Hoboken, NJ: John Wiley & Sons.

Spector, Alan, and Lawrence, Keith. (2010). *Your Retirement Quest: 10 Secrets for Creating and Living a Fulfilling Retirement*. Cincinnati Book Publishers.

Swedroe, Larry, and Berkin, Andrew. (2020). *The Incredible Shrinking Alpha: How to Be a Successful Investor without Picking Winners* (2nd ed.). Petersfield, Hampshire, UK: Harriman House.

Swedroe, Larry, and Grogan, Kevin. (2019). *Your Complete Guide to a Successful and Secure Retirement*. Petersfield, Hampshire, UK: Harriman House.

Zangara, Manuela. (2017). *Homemade Pasta Made Simple: A Pasta Cookbook with Easy Recipes and Lessons to Make Fresh Pasta Any Night*. Berkeley, CA: Rockridge Press.

Index